LISTEN TO THE PEOPLE

A World Bank Publication

The matter of thinking is always confounding—all the more in proportion as we keep clear of prejudice. To keep clear of prejudice, we must be ready and willing to listen. Such readiness allows us to surmount the boundaries in which all customary views are confined, and to reach a more open terrain.

MARTIN HEIDEGGER

LISTEN
TO THE
PEOPLE

**Participant-Observer Evaluation
of Development Projects**

Lawrence F. Salmen

Published for The World Bank
Oxford University Press

327170

Oxford University Press

NEW YORK OXFORD LONDON GLASGOW
TORONTO MELBOURNE WELLINGTON HONG KONG
TOKYO KUALA LUMPUR SINGAPORE JAKARTA
DELHI BOMBAY CALCUTTA MADRAS KARACHI
NAIROBI DAR ES SALAAM CAPE TOWN

First printing January 1987

The World Bank does not accept responsibility for the views
expressed herein, which are those of the author and should not be
attributed to the World Bank or to its affiliated organizations. The
findings, interpretations, and conclusions are the results of research
supported by the Bank; they do not necessarily represent official
policy of the Bank. The designations employed and the presentation
of material in the maps used in this document are solely for the
convenience of the reader and do not imply the expression of any
opinion whatsoever on the part of the World Bank or its affiliates
concerning the legal status of any country, territory, city, area, or of
its authorities, or concerning the delimitation of its boundaries or
national affiliation.

Library of Congress Cataloging-in-Publication Data

Salmen, Lawrence F., 1942–
  Listen to the people.

  Bibliography: p.
  Includes index.
  1. Economic development projects—Bolivia—La Paz—
Evaluation. 2. Economic development projects—
Ecuador—Guayaquil—Evaluation. 3. Economic develop-
ment projects—Developing countries—Evaluation.
I. Title.
HC185.E44S25   1987   338.984'12   86-23672
ISBN 0-19-520545-6

FOREWORD

Development has some dimensions discernible only at ground level. The view from the ground, from where people live and work, is the perspective of this book. Lawrence Salmen spent time living among the people whose lives are affected by two World Bank–supported urban development projects in Latin America. As a neighbor and participant in community life, he gained insights that helped bring about significant improvements in the projects. His application of the techniques of participant observation to the management of development work was then transferred to other projects, and the approach was expanded to include trained observers from the developing countries themselves. These observers are now listening to their own compatriots and thereby stimulating beneficial change in Bank-supported projects in urban and rural areas and in health and population projects elsewhere in Latin America and in Africa and Asia.

The professionals who plan projects and programs are often far removed from the people for whom these activities are intended. The World Bank is interested in incorporating the people's perspective into project work so as to narrow the gap between professionals and the intended beneficiaries. Methods of attending to cultural and behavioral factors—listening to the people—are espoused in this book. They are as important to effective development work as are the more widely recognized tools of financial or economic analysis. As we learn to integrate policies and plans with people's priorities and perspectives, we help bring about processes of sustained development. Directed listening leads to support for the kinds of change that have meaning to the Bank's ultimate clientele—the people who are expected to benefit from the Bank's projects.

S. Shahid Husain
Vice President, Operations Policy
The World Bank

CONTENTS

ACKNOWLEDGMENTS

Many people contributed to this book. The idea of doing a participant-observer evaluation of urban projects originated with David Beckmann in the late 1970s and was heartily endorsed by Anthony Churchill and Harold Dunkerley, all three then working on urban projects at the World Bank. Much of the field research was funded by the Bank's Research Committee. Additional support came from the Bank's Operations Policy staff and from the governments of Bolivia, Brazil, and Ecuador. The evolution from reports to book manuscript was guided at the Bank by a steering committee chaired by Gregory Ingram and consisting of Michael Bamberger, Neil Boyle, Maritta Koch-Weser, and Ian Scott together with the continued active participation of David Beckmann and Harold Dunkerley.

The sponsoring institutions in Bolivia and Ecuador allowed themselves to be exposed to this intensive look by an alien body and were most cooperative at every step of the way. Key individuals in Bolivia were Jaime Medrano and Freddy Quitón of the project implementation agency (HAM-BIRF), Gustavo Medeiros of the Industrial Bank (BISA), and Sammy Vera of the Housing Bank (BANVI); and in Ecuador, Enrique Blacio and Sandra Luque of the Housing Bank (BEV), Jaime Vera and Nelly Valarezo of the municipality of Guayaquil, and Alexis de Aguilar and Rafael Cuesta of the Banco del Pacífico.

A number of experts in urban development from Latin America and the United States were kind enough to read and comment on the initial reports that served as the basis for Part I of this book. From Brazil were Vilma Faria, Carlos Nelson, Lenina Pomeranz, and Ephim Schluger; from Mexico, María Elena Colcero and Leonel Lechuga; from Peru, José Matos Mar; and from the United States, primarily Anthony Leeds and Lisa Peattie. All of them had a particular interest in applying research effectively to action.

Special recognition is due to my research assistants, Yolanda Barriga and Luisa Fernanda Rada in La Paz and Hilda Sánchez de Gaviria in Guayaquil. They effectively applied their formal training in economics and sociology to obtain a grounded understanding of their low-income compatriots and to pave the way for the later application of the approach to other localities.

Two individuals provided invaluable assistance with the text itself. Sheryl Mattingly painstakingly reviewed each chapter with an eye to conceptual clarity. John Dinges later performed a similar function, this time for clarity of expression.

Interpreting another people's perception of reality in the dynamic context of a development project and communicating that perception to third parties, host-country managers, and Bank officials is fraught with risk. A select group of persons sensitive to the needs and wants of one or more of the publics concerned provided a most appreciated service of reading reports or chapters to help indicate whether I was on course or foundering. For their encouragement and helpful guidance I thank William Carmichael, Michael Cernea, Jean-Loup Dherse, Peter Hakim, Richard Heaver, Arturo Israel, Ragnar Overby, Katherine and David Sommers, and Roberto Zagha. Particular appreciation is felt for Stanley Salmen as counselor, critic, father, and friend.

Credit for the meticulous work of typing—at all hours—goes to Morallina George, Suzana de Jesus, and Jocelyn Milord.

Ultimately of most significance were the hundreds of people with whom I conversed—in their homes, at their places of work, and in community meetings. These people, particularly those with whom I came to share close friendship—the families of Laura Zeballos and Gabriel Llayuno—were the window through which I came to see the people's project world. By opening that world to me, they enabled me to listen closely to the people and they brought the projects to life.

<< **1** >>

THE PARTICIPANT OBSERVER

The Neighborhood Committee of 8 de Diciembre, a settlement of low-income families in La Paz, Bolivia, holds its weekly meetings in a small and dimly lit one-room building. At a meeting I attended in early March 1982, there was barely room for the dozen or so men present. Some were seated around three sides of a small desk, others were standing or squatting on the cement floor. The men were in the midst of an intense discussion about the government project to improve their neighborhood. They displayed mixed emotions of pride and dissatisfaction. They were proud to be part of a development effort that had transformed alleys into streets and wastelands into playing fields; the dreary look of poverty was gone, and their settlement was now a well-serviced urban area with direct water and sewerage connections to the houses. It was one of the few low-income communities of the Bolivian capital to have access to such services.

Yet there had been delays—one of those present pointed out that even though the municipal project should have been completed months ago, some families were still without water and sewer hookups. "The people working on the project are too distant from us," he said. He and others kept returning to the same point: the project was not charity; they, the residents of the improved area, were paying for what they received. For that very reason, they felt, the project staff should pay attention to the wishes and preferences of those who lived in the community. The president of the Neighborhood Committee summed up the core of the issue:

The municipality and the World Bank are doing a good project here. We are at last becoming a part of the city proper. Now we are respectable people [*somos gente*]. But we need to be heard. The project is changing our homes, our neighborhood, our very way of life. There should be a directorate overseeing this project with equal representation from both the municipality and the community. We should also have trained personnel—engineers and accountants—who are directly responsible to the community. They would review the municipal plans and implementation procedures and suggest corrections where needed. After all, we are paying for this project. We have a right to be heard.

As the president sat down, I sensed a certain embarrassment—but not disagreement—on the part of others in the room. He had been perhaps too frank, his criticisms too direct in the presence of a foreign visitor (I had been introduced as someone evaluating the project on behalf of the World Bank, which was providing funding for the project). Their message, however, could not have been clearer: in their eyes the project was a good one, but it had important problems. They were frustrated that the project managers did not see the problems as they did—and, even worse, that the project managers had not consulted the residents about the problems.

What had gone wrong? The men in that room that evening were not hesitant to talk. The project by all accounts had made improvements. The Neighborhood Committee and personnel implementing the project had made efforts to communicate with one another. There had been regular meetings of residents and municipal staff, and letters had been exchanged. Yet the people felt that their opinions and feelings about the project had not been taken seriously. To them, the channels of communication seemed weak, and there was no way to get their point of view across to the professionals who were changing their lives.

The evening's discussion shed light on the two worlds that meet, not always smoothly, in projects intended to improve low-income communities in developing countries: the world of the project beneficiaries and that of the professionals—in and outside the country—whose job is to design and execute development projects. People at the grass roots of society who are the ultimate beneficiaries of loan programs have a point of view distinct from that of executing agencies or loan agencies. Yet their voice often does not reach administrators and managers, who could use the beneficiaries' perspective in the design, execution, and monitoring of projects. The world of the professionals consists of written forms, budgetary constraints, and other bureaucratic exigencies. Most of the activity in their world takes place in the offices and corridors of a particular agency. Rarely do they go out into the world being affected by the decisions they make.

How can persons of one world effectively plan and manage activities for people of the other without understanding them on their own terms? Development projects would be more effective if they better incorporated the point of view of the people who are the intended beneficiaries. Aren't there ways for persons entrusted with development funds to listen to the people they are trying to help? Can't professionals go to the people where they live and work and learn to perceive their needs and their own ideas about how they would improve their lives? Wouldn't development professionals themselves benefit from such listening? And might not this listening stance lead to more open, integrated societies where people and professionals are less remote from one another?

These were the questions on my mind as I visited that meeting of neighbors in La Paz, and they remain the questions that underlie this book.

« »

The assignment that led me to that meeting and to dozens like it in La Paz and in Guayaquil, Ecuador, began with a disarmingly simple telephone call from a World Bank staff member in mid-1979. "We want you to go and live with project beneficiaries in low-income areas of two Latin American cities to gain an understanding of the projects from their point of view," he said. Two years later the invitation was made formal. In early 1982 I began to conduct a participant-observer evaluation of World Bank–assisted urban projects in the two cities. Although both projects comprised diverse components, in La Paz the evaluation focused on the upgrading of an existing community; in Guayaquil I resided in a new low-cost housing project and became familiar with an adjacent community which had resisted upgrading for reasons unclear to local and World Bank managers. The method used, which I have designated participant-observer evaluation, is a new way of evaluating World Bank projects and should be applicable to development activities generally. The method evolved during my residence in the low-income communities that were the project sites. I lived in each city for four months initially, followed by additional stays of three months in each. The total time of the evaluation, including report writing, was nineteen months.

This book is, in essence, an account of what I found as I observed large development projects from the inside. In addition, it describes attempts to apply the methodology elsewhere in both urban and rural projects using host-country professionals to carry out the evaluation. It also reports on the participant-observer evaluation method itself, on its advantages and pitfalls in the design and management of projects.

The assignment and the development of the participant-observer evaluation method grew out of a concern in the World Bank to improve the execution of its urban projects. The Bank began lending to help developing countries cope with the problems of urban poverty and rapid urban growth in the early 1970s. Its approach was frankly experimental and was often referred to as a process of "learning by doing." The Bank intended its urban projects to pioneer new approaches, which developing countries could emulate with their own resources.

In many countries governments were providing subsidized housing for relatively well-off people, while the urban poor crowded into squatter settlements, often in unhealthy environments such as swamps and ravines, with little or no infrastructure or services such as water and electricity. By contrast, the World Bank financed housing (sometimes only serviced lots where poor people could build their own homes) that was within the reach of genuinely low-income families. The Bank insisted that beneficiaries of its shelter projects should pay over time for the infrastructure and housing they received. This cost-recovery policy made it possible for public authorities to undertake similar programs on the scale needed to reach the vast numbers of people lacking adequate housing. No government can afford to subsidize housing for all low-income people, and the World Bank was pushing for an approach that could eventually improve conditions for all the urban poor.

In nearly all developing countries, public authorities tend to ignore squatter settlements. In the early 1970s some governments still resorted to occasional programs of slum clearance. By contrast, the World Bank financed programs to upgrade slums, to increase access to services, and to raise health and safety to minimum levels. The programs encouraged cost recovery so that the programs could be repeated on a larger scale. The Bank also experimented with programs to provide credit and technical assistance to some of the many small, informal businesses that are characteristically found among the urban poor.[1]

From the beginning of the Bank's urban work, provisions were made for learning the views of beneficiaries. The desirability and advantages of such information for project design and implementation were obvious. How best to determine participant views, evaluate their significance, and use that information appropriately to modify projects was less obvious. Traditional sample surveys, for example, provide relevant data, but they are relatively expensive and the questionnaires are often intimidating to poor people confronted by an unknown interrogator. Moreover, such surveys often fail to reveal the motives underlying the views expressed. And the formulation of written questionnaires presupposes prior knowledge by project managers about significant problem areas and the preferences of beneficiaries. There are similar disadvantages to holding formal discussions among community representatives—who may be far from representative—and project managers. Both groups often have hidden agendas that prevent a frank and accurate exchange of views.

The Bank, in common with other development agencies, experimented over the years with various approaches to improving communication between project agencies and beneficiaries. Before work began on the Bank's first urban effort, a housing project in Dakar, Senegal, a sociological study was undertaken to learn "felt needs" of possible participants and to facilitate the assignment of homogeneous groups to the new neighborhoods. In an early Lusaka, Zambia, upgrading scheme, "walking groups" of participants accompanied the managers around the site to determine the alignment of roads and pathways. In the Dandora community project in Nairobi, Kenya, a small team of observers from a local university paid periodic visits to the project area to talk with participants and highlight particular difficulties that arose in the course of project implementation.

The evaluation of development assistance has often been overly oriented toward abstract indices of change that are of limited use to the project practitioner. Traditional impact evaluations consist of before-and-after measurements of such project effects as changes in income or health. These changes, however, are generally of insignificant magnitude and are difficult to ascribe primarily to a particular intervention. Moreover, traditional evaluations fail to address issues that arise during the course of project implementation, such as the degree of communication between beneficiaries and management, they do not shed light on community power relations that might determine who has access to the benefits of the project, and they generally do not reveal the values and behavior of beneficiaries.

The development of the participant-observer evaluation method and my assignment to live on the project sites in La Paz and Guayaquil were attempts to remedy these shortcomings and to take the valuable insights of experiments such as that at Dandora one step further. The basic idea was to learn as much about the projects as possible from the perspective of the beneficiaries by means of participant observation, an anthropological technique whereby a trained observer gains insight from personal involvement in a social setting. Arrangements were made with two project agencies in Ecuador and Bolivia for me to live in project communities for varying periods, to participate in local activities, and to develop new approaches and methodologies for improving communication between the participants and those sharing responsibility for the projects.

I spent the following two years bringing together the diverse perspectives of residents of the project areas and of project managers. I resided in the project sites and recruited local assistants to help verify my impressions. Some of the time was spent away from the communities to reflect on the information and formulate reports. Project components, such as credit programs, that did not lend themselves to on-site participant observation were evaluated through a series of qualitative interviews—guided informal conversations that allow respondents to express in their own terms what a project means to them.

Participant-observer evaluation as described in this book is an eclectic blend of techniques designed to interpret the real world of the intended project beneficiaries—their perceived needs, hopes, and frustrations—so as to contribute to the decisionmaking needs of project managers. Decisionmakers thereby receive feedback they can use to improve the projects they are currently working on. Evaluators sound out the opinions and reactions of the people who are expected to benefit from the project interventions. The subject matter for interviews is selected by project management. Interviews are conducted in an open, conversational style, both to establish rapport and to allow unforeseen, yet pertinent, subjects to enter into the discussion. The emphasis is on creating a relationship of trust between evaluator and beneficiary. Once elicited, the people's interpretation of a project is expressed descriptively and, wherever possible, numerically as well.

Participant-observer evaluation is done quickly enough to be of use in improving the project, but it needs enough time to avoid superficiality. Qualitative interviews with a sample of beneficiaries around project-related topics usually take no more than two or three weeks. Residence in a community need not exceed three months. Direct observation, including the simple counting of project effects, may complement these qualitative procedures. But participant-observer evaluation does not entail elaborate statistical computations that require a high degree of expertise and sophisticated computer hardware, neither of which is readily available in many developing countries.

Managers may use participant-observer evaluation as a tool at various points in a project cycle. Before an intervention this guided, cultural sounding of the population may be used to learn the community's basic values and behavior patterns, around which a program or project will be designed. As exemplified in this book, participant-observer evaluation may also be used to monitor the interaction between the project and its beneficiaries so that project management can take ongoing self-corrective action. Obtaining honest, in-depth reactions of beneficiaries may also be useful as a trouble-shooting device to resolve particular problems during implementation. After a project is completed the techniques may be used to assess whether the benefits have been sustained and what indirect effects the project may have produced over time.

Not only was the World Bank interested in the method of participant-observer evaluation itself, it also wanted to know if the method could be done by persons in developing countries with minimal direction from the Bank. The question was, first, whether incorporating the point of view of project beneficiaries into management decisionmaking in this way was useful and cost-effective. If it proved successful, then the question was whether professionals in developing countries would be willing and able to cross class and income lines so as to interpret the perspective of project beneficiaries of their own society and provide useful feedback to host-country and Bank managers. On the basis of the experiment in La Paz and Guayaquil, the Bank decided to use the approach in urban areas in Brazil and Thailand and in rural communities in the Bolivian Altiplano.

The premise of this book is that there is a way to learn about people undergoing development that may provoke direct and immediate benefits to them. Wherever participant observers looked closely—at housing projects in Thailand, fishing cooperatives in Brazil, or agricultural endeavors in Bolivia—they found areas of concern that transcend sectoral and regional differences. This intense observation revealed that many people simply do not understand the nature of the projects intended to benefit them. Often there are established local interests—political leaders or entrepreneurs—whose influence on the beneficiaries has been ignored or underestimated. Project components are often viewed out of context, as isolated abstractions in and of themselves rather than as interventions affecting people who have unique histories, locations, and cultures.

When project designers and managers listen to the people, however, their projects can be made to appeal to what people value, to reinforce people's own identity, and to enhance their self-respect. When this happens, when a project touches the inner core of beneficiaries, it becomes a catalyst for self-improvement and the development it achieves becomes self-generating.

Participant-observer evaluation is not an entirely new concept. As elaborated in chapter 7 it is akin to process, illuminative, responsive, and other types of evaluation developed largely in the United States since the mid-1960s. What is relatively new, however, is the application of this blend of both qualitative and quantitative techniques to the better understanding of international development projects. This approach is long overdue inasmuch as primarily statistical, quantitative analyses of social and economic phenomena are particularly inappropriate in developing countries where the data base is poor and the need for cultural, contextual understanding is great. This book is the story of how an appreciation of people on their own terms led to decisions which improved these people's living conditions. The World Bank supported this participant-observer evaluation as an experiment, and the approach continues to evolve in new regions and new sectors. It is presented here to encourage others to join in building the bridge of understanding between professionals and the poor in development projects, both within and between countries. Without this understanding no amount of technical assistance or capital will provide effective development.

The organization of this book reflects the evolution of the approach. Part I discusses the first phase of the experiment, the work of structured observation in La Paz and Guayaquil. Chapter 2 describes the low-income communities that were the sites of the projects and my living arrangements in those communities. This is the only largely descriptive chapter of the book. It provides the setting for the participant-observer experience related in the subsequent chapters of Part I, which present the findings and insights of the hybrid qualitative-quantitative approach with regard to communication, the catalytic effects of development, and the contexts of the two projects. Part II discusses the transferability of the approach and its precepts. Chapter 6 describes the second phase of the experiment, in which the method of participant-observer evaluation was used in other project areas and other countries where primary responsibility for the approach lay with host-country personnel. The participant-observer evaluation method itself is elaborated in chapter 7. The concluding chapter summarizes the significance of participant-observer evaluation as a tool for project management and as a legitimate development activity in its own right.

« PART I »

Experimentation in La Paz and Guayaquil

« 2 »

PROJECTS AND PLACES

It would be difficult to pick two major cities of Latin America more dissimilar in physical setting than La Paz, Bolivia, and Guayaquil, Ecuador. La Paz is a picturesque capital city located in the high Altiplano of the Andes Mountains. Guayaquil is an unprepossessing tropical port bordering on marshes and swampy estuaries. La Paz, as the seat of the Bolivian government, is the center of the country's political life. Guayaquil, as Ecuador's commercial and financial center, has economic importance. Both cities are the largest in their respective countries, La Paz with a population of roughly 800,000 and Guayaquil with about 1,200,000.

Like most major urban places of the developing world, both cities have been growing rapidly—La Paz at average annual rates of 3.5 percent and Guayaquil at 5 percent over the past twenty years. Roughly a third of each city's population is made up of migrants, many of whom, especially in La Paz, retain close ties to family members in the countryside. The migrants join large numbers of persons in both cities already living in poorly serviced, unsanitary accommodations. According to rough estimates, over a third of La Paz's population and at least half of the inhabitants of Guayaquil live in houses lacking water or sewer connections, or both.

The two projects I was to evaluate were intended to remedy these problems. Together the projects were to provide roughly 42,000 low-income families with better services, improved housing, or new jobs. The World Bank loaned a total of $48 million to the governments of Bolivia and Ecuador to support the efforts.[1]

The two projects were broadly similar. Each included programs of new low-cost housing (sites and services or core housing), slum upgrading, and credit to small-scale enterprises. In both countries, the new housing under construction was the least expensive housing ever built or authorized by public authorities, and the programs of slum upgrading and credit for small-scale enterprises were unprecedented in scale. The World Bank's policy of full cost recovery was also a sharp departure from previous practice in both countries, which had heavily subsidized projects for the urban poor.

The projects were ambitious, remarkably focused on the poor, and innovative in almost all respects. The components of the projects and the eight government agencies involved are specified in table 1.

Table 1. World Bank Project Components, La Paz and Guayaquil

Component	Scale	Implementing agency	Cost (millions of dollars)
La Paz			
Upgrading	About 7,000 families	Municipality (HAM)	8.2
New housing	2,000 units (and 6 hectares industrial sites)	National Housing Council (CONAVI)	7.6
	400 units	Housing Bank (BANVI)	2.3
Credit programs	About 200 artisans (and 10 hectares industrial sites)	Industrial Bank (BISA)	5.2
Health	Child care for low-income areas	Ministry of Health	1.2
Subtotal			24.5
Guayaquil			
Upgrading	About 3,400 families	Municipality	8.4
New housing	About 3,200 sites	Municipality	6.9
	504 units	Housing Bank (BEV)	1.6
Credit programs	About 6,400 home improvement loans for upgrading and sites and services	Municipality	8.8
	3,000 home improvement loans in existing low-income settlements	Housing Bank (BEV)	3.9
	About 6,400 loans to 5,300 artisans	Banco del Pacífico	9.0
Subtotal			38.6
Total[a]			63.1

a. The total figure does not include contingencies ($10.8 million) or costs of technical assistance, project units, and other amounts difficult to allocate by program ($2.2 million).

The government of Bolivia and the World Bank signed a loan agreement for the La Paz urban project in late 1977. By 1982, when the evaluation began, much of the project had been implemented. The most successful component of the Bolivia project was slum upgrading. The implementation agency of the project was a special department, known as HAM-BIRF,[2] within the municipality of La Paz. The same agency, together with the Banco Industrial, S.A. (BISA), administered the credit to small-scale enterprises, another successful component of the project. The new housing component, however, was plagued by administrative problems and delays. In 1980, largely because of these delays, the government of Bolivia and the World Bank restructured the project to expand the successful components and reduce the new housing component.

I lived for five months in 8 de Diciembre, one of the barrios, or neighborhoods, being upgraded. My time there was divided into two periods, of three and two months, separated by an interval of eight months. I spent most of my time in La Paz getting to know the people of my own neighborhood. The rest of my time was spent learning about other neighborhoods affected by the upgrading program, interviewing small-scale entrepreneurs who had received credit from the project, and interviewing future occupants of the new housing being built with the assistance from the project. During a typical week I would try to spend evenings and the weekend—when heads of households were most apt to be home—in the barrio, visiting friends and attending meetings, formal and informal. Weekdays would be spent writing notes (in the morning) and conducting interviews, informal or structured, following a pre-established list of topics.

My local assistants and I conducted five formal surveys in La Paz. Soon after I settled into my rental quarters in 8 de Diciembre we administered a socioeconomic questionnaire to a representative sample of the people of that barrio. We later conducted two in-depth qualitative surveys of representative residents of the barrio, one during each period of residence. The intent of each was to gauge people's satisfaction with the upgrading project, assess their relations with project implementation staff and with their own Neighborhood Committee, and determine what changes in their lives had been provoked by the project. The other two surveys were also qualitative, and both were administered during my first stay. One assessed the value of the credit program to the artisans, and the other investigated the motivation for moving to the public housing project. We interviewed samples of artisans and home buyers in their places of work and residence, respectively, in virtually all the major low-income neighborhoods of La Paz.

In Guayaquil, the World Bank was helping to finance one section of a large low-cost housing project called Floresta in the southern part of the city. Although the government of Ecuador and the Bank had signed the loan agreement in late 1980, there had been delays here as well, and the project was only beginning to have a significant effect when I arrived in 1982. In addition, the implementing agency, the Ecuadorian Housing Bank (BEV), was for the first time making credit available for home improvements in low-income neighborhoods. Loans for small-scale enterprises were another component of the Guayaquil project and an expansion of a program pioneered by a commercial bank, the Banco del Pacífico. The project also included a slum improvement and sites-and-services component under the administration of the municipality of Guayaquil. It was originally planned for Guasmo Norte but was shifted to Guasmo Fertisa, both squatter settlements on the southern fringe of Guayaquil.

I lived for five months in the Housing Bank's low-cost housing project in Floresta. I divided my time in Guayaquil fairly evenly among the Floresta project, the home improvement and small-scale enterprise credit programs, and an exploration of why the municipality's first attempt at slum upgrading failed. As in La Paz, I lived in Guayaquil during two periods, of four and three months, separated by an interval of seven months.

In Guayaquil I conducted six formal surveys, again with the help of local research assistants. These fell on various points along the spectrum from quantitative, closed questionnaire to qualitative, open, unstructured interview. The two credit programs, for artisans and home improvements, were addressed by questionnaire-like interview forms containing a mixture of closed and open questions, which were used with representative samples of the two groups at their places of work and residence, respectively, in all the major low-income areas of Guayaquil. In Floresta, where I lived, we talked with residents in a less structured way about their adjustment to the new housing, their home improvements, and their attitudes toward their local elected representative. In addition, we asked future residents of the World Bank–supported section of Floresta (which was not yet inhabited during my first stay) about their reasons for moving to Floresta. The least structured interviews were conducted in Guasmo Norte, to ask why the people thought the slum improvement project had not been executed in their area, and in Guasmo Fertisa, to ascertain the people's willingness to pay for, and their general attitude toward, the similar project which was expected to take place in their community.

In each of the cities I recruited local assistants to help with the evaluation work. Part of the initial experiment was to see whether local persons could be trained to perform this kind of qualitative research effectively. In addition it was expected that local persons would provide me with a contextual orientation I lacked and serve as checks on my own impressions about elements of the programs they would look at from their own unique perspective. I was fortunate to encounter three well-qualified assistants who accompanied me during the entire course of this experimental phase: Yolanda Barriga and Luisa Fernanda Rada, sociologists in La Paz, and Hilda Sánchez de Gaviria, an economist in Guayaquil. All three had completed university training and had several years of experience conducting surveys among the low-income urban population in their own cities. Each of these assistants participated in the formal surveys and lived in a project area for three months.[3] The chiefs of the evaluation and social offices of the project executing units in La Paz and Guayaquil, Freddy Quitón and Rodrigo Trujillo, also participated on a part-time basis, Quitón by living in a project area of La Paz and Trujillo by conducting interviews with artisans. This experience helped instill an understanding of this evaluation method in the project unit itself. Several other local part-time interviewers were engaged in each city.

I learned about these two urban development projects by sharing in the life of 8 de Diciembre and Floresta, by talking with my neighbors, and by interviewing and having informal discussions with the beneficiaries of these and other project components. I also read project documents and interviewed project administrators and World Bank staff in order to learn their points of view. But my focus was always on the experience of the people for whom these projects were intended.

La Paz

La Paz is a dramatic city, unlike any other major urban area in appearance. From the air it looks like an inclined wide-lipped oval bowl; running along much of its base is a seam, or ridge—a line of skyscrapers comprising the modern downtown area. Two-thirds of La Paz's population of 800,000 reside within the bowl and up the sides (*laderas*), with upper-class neighborhoods at the lowest point. The top edge of the bowl, El Alto, is part of the Altiplano Plateau and the site of mixed low-income residential and industrial uses. The city is given additional character by the nearby majestic mountain, Illimani, which looks over it from a height of more than 6,200 meters, or 20,400 feet.

La Paz is the country's capital and largest city with 14 percent of the country's population in 1976. It produces more than half of the gross national product (GNP) of Bolivia and has 45 percent of the nation's employment in the industrial sector. Yet only about a third of La Paz's economically active population are in the industrial sector, and of these less than a quarter work in companies with more than twenty employees.[4] The rest make their living as artisans and in small-scale businesses. The top fifth of the income scale earn 65 percent of all income while the lowest fifth earn less than 3 percent.[5]

About a third of the people of La Paz are Indians who have come from small communities of the Altiplano, bringing with them their distinctive Aymara language and culture, dress and customs.[6] The migrants maintain close ties to the countryside. Almost three-quarters (72 percent) of the migrants return to their place of origin at least once a year, and 23 percent return at least once a month.[7] More than any other major city of Latin America, La Paz is a meeting place for indigenous and European cultures, and much of the transition from one to the other is made in the downtown tenements and barrios.

The people of La Paz are for the most part poor. The average monthly household income in La Paz in 1976 was 6,100 pesos. By January of 1982 estimates placed this at 7,100 pesos ($170). A series of devaluations beginning in February 1982 caused household income to deteriorate in dollar terms. By April 1983, at the end of my second stay in La Paz, average monthly household income, which I estimated very roughly in nominal terms to be 16,000 pesos, was worth only $40. The consumer price index for the same period rose about 300 percent,[8] while salaries rose at less than half that rate and rose especially slowly among nonunionized workers (more than 80 percent of the work force of La Paz).[9]

Although I was aware of the statistics on the Bolivian economy, my day-to-day observations of changes affecting friends and neighbors in the low-income project area of 8 de Diciembre were more telling. One woman had taken out a loan to rebuild a wall that had been torn down in order to widen the road as part of the upgrading . She had missed four monthly payments of 380 pesos ($8.60) because her working husband had not been paid for three of those months. Similar stories were told by other residents. Artisans faced increasing hardships as the prices of imported raw materials, tools, and machinery skyrocketed while the demand for their services decreased. Families consumed less and less of relatively costly foods, such as meat and eggs, and more of the staples of the Andean diet, principally potatoes. By the middle of 1983 the effects of a countrywide drought were felt in La Paz as increasing numbers of non-Spanish-speaking highland peasants appeared along the sidewalks in the center of the city awkwardly asking for humiliating but necessary handouts.

Housing is important to the people of La Paz both as shelter and as a symbol. The climate of La Paz is often inclement, with heavy rains from November to March, temperatures below freezing, and cold winds on the hillsides and the Altiplano where most of the poor live. Houses in La Paz need a sturdy exterior. Building material is often adobe, with roofs of corrugated aluminum. The shacks of plywood, cardboard, and odd bits of refuse found in many cities of other Latin American countries are not in evidence in La Paz. In addition, walls dividing one resident's lot from another are important to preserve privacy. A person's identity appears to be more closely connected to his home and neighborhood than is the case in most cities.

Both the quantity and the quality of housing in La Paz are deficient. The government built less than 1,000 units a year through the 1970s, and privately built houses cost far more than the majority are able to pay. Most La Paz families therefore build their own housing, and most of what they build is poorly serviced and too small. Density is high, averaging more than two persons per habitable room among the 72 percent of the city's population living in the low-income unserviced neighborhoods.[10]

Because of the steep inclines of La Paz and the area's ecological function as a catchment for the Altiplano, 185 small streams run down the sides of the bowl, and much of the land is subject to floods and landslides. In 1979 the municipality of La Paz estimated that 84 percent of the houses of the city were built on land that is unstable because of underground or exposed rivers or on steep inclines subject to landslides.[11] This helps explain why more than a third of all houses are not connected to piped water. In low-income areas (primarily on the laderas and El Alto) this figure jumps to 86 percent. More than three-quarters of the people in these areas get their water from public taps. More than one in ten families in the poor neighborhoods get their water from generally unsanitary sources such as rivers, drainage ditches, and stagnant pools. A third of the city's total population have no sewer connection. In the poor areas of the city, where most of the city's population lives, this figure rises to 89 percent. Electricity, however, is well provided, with only 14 percent lacking it citywide and 17 percent in the poorer areas.[12] The World Bank's first loan for urban projects in 1977 was intended to meet some of these needs.

In the southwestern portion of the bowl of La Paz, about three-quarters up from the base to the top, is the neighborhood of 8 de Diciembre (see map 1). It is a part of the larger region of Sopocachi, a venerable, staid community of middle- and upper-class families. The project area is separated from its elegant neighbor by the Cotahuma River, a foul-smelling

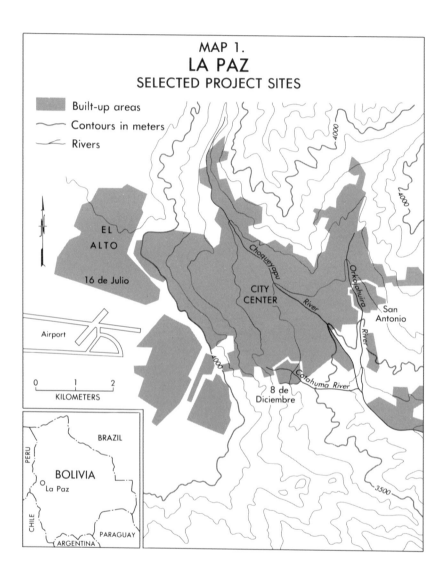

MAP 1.
LA PAZ
SELECTED PROJECT SITES

Built-up areas
Contours in meters
Rivers

EL ALTO

16 de Julio

Airport

CITY CENTER

Choqueyapu River

Orkojahuira River

San Antonio

8 de Diciembre

Cotahuma River

4000

4000

3500

4000

0   1   2
KILOMETERS

BRAZIL

PERU

BOLIVIA

○ La Paz

CHILE

PARAGUAY

ARGENTINA

running latrine and open garbage pit bordering 8 de Diciembre on the north and east. The river frequently floods and changes its course, spreading filth and causing the area to be badly suited for construction. Another river, the Duraznani (also known as the Jinchupalla), smaller but similarly unclean, runs along the southern border of the community. At the highest point, to the west, a series of steps separates 8 de Diciembre Alto from another marginal community.

Despite its disadvantages the residents of 8 de Diciembre consider it a most pleasant and convenient place to live. Adjacent to one of the most esteemed residential neighborhoods of La Paz, it is only a half hour by foot and 15 minutes by bus from downtown. In addition, the community has an excellent view of Illimani across the bowl to the east.

As recently as twenty-five years ago, the 700-hectare area that is now 8 de Diciembre was largely open land cultivated for truck farming or left as pasturage for sheep and cattle. The entire area was owned by six or seven well-off families. As migration and natural population growth pushed La Paz outward and upward, the owners sold the land in lots, at considerable profit, to residents of nearby urban areas who sought to escape rising rents. All of the area's residents came from other parts of La Paz. Of the 100 families in 8 de Diciembre that my assistants and I interviewed in March 1982, more than half (52 percent) had previously lived less than five kilometers away; another quarter (28 percent) came from areas only five to ten kilometers away. The new urban settlement was founded on April 18, 1965, as the zone of 8 de Diciembre. By naming their community for the Roman Catholic Feast of the Immaculate Conception (December 8), which is celebrated as a local religious holiday in Sopocachi, the early residents were not only demonstrating their faith but forging a desired link with the prestigious community of Sopocachi.

Although most of the burgeoning population of this new area was poor, it always included a small but influential minority of middle-class families who had inherited land from one of the original landowners or had chosen 8 de Diciembre for its semipastoral, picturesque setting, low land costs, and relative proximity to the center of La Paz.

According to local leaders and municipal officials, these middle-class families had begun pressing the municipality for urban improvements, sewerage and water in particular, as early as 1971, fully eight years before the project began. The first recorded evidence of such activity is a series of letters in August and September 1977 from the Junta de Vecinos (Neighborhood Committee) of 8 de Diciembre to the municipality's director of community action, to the president of the Federation of Neighborhood

Committees, and to the mayor of La Paz. The letters asked for "urbaniza-tion," especially sewerage, and indicated the readiness of the neighborhood to pay for whatever improvements were made and to contribute their own labor to help with the execution of the work.

More and more families arrived in 8 de Diciembre throughout the 1970s, buying plots and constructing homes or, in increasing numbers, renting. By December 1979, at the beginning of the project, it is estimated that approxi-mately 700 families lived in 8 de Diciembre. Of these only slightly more than 200 had signed contracts with the municipality promising to pay for project improvements. (Why such a small portion of the area's population signed up for the project will be discussed at greater length below.)

Inasmuch as there were no good, recent socioeconomic data on the people of 8 de Diciembre, in early March 1982 we applied a questionnaire to a randomly selected sample of 100 families (roughly, every seventh house) in the central and upper parts of the area to obtain a general description of the population, from which later, more in-depth soundings could be made. The findings of this survey confirmed that 8 de Diciembre was much like other peripheral or marginal areas of La Paz, though some-what more heterogeneous: it contained a small but important number of middle-class families whereas other low-income areas generally do not.

The survey showed that the people of 8 de Diciembre were for the most part poor, nuclear families. Although they had lived in this neighborhood for as long as twenty years, most still lived in overcrowded dwellings without access to city sewerage or water systems. Both the community and its households were stable. Nuclear families outnumbered extended fami-lies in a ratio of seven to three. Heads of family had lived in 8 de Diciembre for an average of eleven years; 90 percent were male and averaged 44 years of age. More than half (52 percent) of heads of households were born in La Paz, the rest averaged twenty-eight years' residence in the city. As further indication of the relative urbanism of the people of 8 de Diciembre, 60 percent of the total population surveyed spoke only Spanish, the other 40 percent spoke both Spanish and Aymara or Quechua, or all three.[13] As is true of the entire Bolivian population, the people of 8 de Diciembre were young; the median age of the population sampled was twenty-one. Each household averaged 1.7 wage earners and had four dependents. Forty-one percent of the wives were wage earners, most of whom (56 percent) worked part-time.

The range of income reported in the survey was wide. The poorest third of 8 de Diciembre's households earned roughly 25,000 pesos a year (less than about $950). The top fifth of the sample earned more than three times this amount. During the time of this study, early 1982 to mid-1983, the Bolivian economy deteriorated rapidly. Not only did nominal rises in salary not keep pace with the increasing cost of living, but unemployment and underemployment increased as factories laid off workers and self-employed artisans lost customers. In 8 de Diciembre the average monthly household income of 7,900 pesos in January 1982 translated into $200; according to rough estimates of my own it was about 12,000 pesos in April of 1983, an equivalent of $24. By mid-1983 there was little meat to be found on the tables of 8 de Diciembre residents, and many of the men had to replace beer with the cheaper but more injurious local grain alcohol (*chicha*).

Of heads of households, 10 percent were illiterate and 41 percent had only a primary school education or less. Only 15 percent had completed secondary school, mostly those in the top income-earning group. A third of these (5 percent of the total) had gone beyond secondary level to a technical institute or university. It is this 15 percent that comprises the important middle-class element of 8 de Diciembre.

About 700 families lived on as many hectares; the residents of this neighborhood had twice as much external space as the average for La Paz.[14] Because families in 8 de Diciembre were large and poor, however, houses tended to be more crowded: an average of 5.7 persons per family and 3.0 persons per room, compared with 1976 census figures for La Paz of 4.1 persons per family and 2.3 persons per room.

The high internal densities and lack of urban services, together with the high altitude and sometimes harsh climate, had adversely affected the health of area residents. Child mortality, an excellent barometer of health conditions, was high in 8 de Diciembre. According to the survey of 100 families, 22 of 106 children born in the five years preceding the survey had died. Reasons for death were largely environmental and related to high-density living: respiratory ailments, measles, scarlet fever, and gastroenteritis.

My place of residence in 8 de Diciembre was a one-room dwelling originally intended to be a store. The owners, Jaime and María, a middle-aged couple with five young children, lived in a three-room house on the same lot. The couple did not have the capital to buy inventory for the store and so were happy to rent it to me. The house was centrally located in the barrio of 8 de Diciembre (see map 2) and opened onto a small garden of daisies and roses. From the windows I could see Illimani. The room was small (nine by fifteen feet), with a cement floor that got very cold at night. For the first month there were no sanitary facilities. Cold water from a nearby well was supplied by a spigot near my door. Once the latrine was built and an

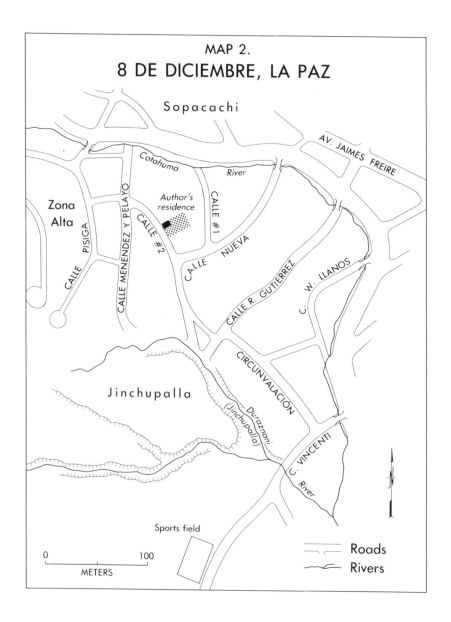

MAP 2.
8 DE DICIEMBRE, LA PAZ

Sopacachi

AV. JAIMES FREIRE

Cotahuma

River

Zona
Alta

CALLE MENÉNDEZ Y PELAYO

CALLE PISIGA

CALLE #2

CALLE #1

Author's
residence

CALLE NUEVA

CALLE R. GUTIERREZ

C. W. LLANOS

CIRCUNVALACIÓN

Jinchupalla

Duraznani
(Jinchupalla)

C. VINCENTI

C. River

Sports field

0   100

METERS

——— Roads
~~~ Rivers

electric heater and rugs purchased, I lived in relative comfort and beauty during my stay in La Paz.

Guayaquil

Guayaquil is a city growing beyond its means and showing its dynamism more by contrast than by unity. Modern buildings rise out of a decaying, formless urban core. Vast tracts of bamboo shacks proliferate into and over the marshy lands and tidal estuaries that surround much of the city. Half of Guayaquil's 1.2 million inhabitants live in these wet areas. Guayaquil has roughly a third of the country's urban population and has been growing at an average annual rate of approximately 5 percent since 1930, when the city's population was only 116,000.[15] The growth was fed by migration as a result of decreasing employment opportunities in agriculture and increasing opportunities in the city, generated in part by Ecuador's import substitution policies begun in 1950. Since the late 1970s, 30 percent of Guayaquil's annual population growth has been made up of migrants.[16] Roughly three-quarters of the migrants in the low-income communities of Guayaquil come from coastal provinces, the remainder from the Sierra.[17] Over a third (37 percent) of Guayaquil's labor force is made up of migrants.[18]

Guayaquil accounts for half of the nation's industrial consumption of electricity and nearly as much (42 percent) of the country's gross value of industrial production, almost double the corresponding figures for Quito, the second largest city.[19] A fifth of Guayaquil's labor force worked in industry in 1977, the majority (54 percent) in services and commerce.[20]

Guayaquil is made up of disparate, quite individualized urban agglomerations (map 3). In the past the poor lived in overcrowded apartments in downtown slums called *tugurios*. Beginning in the mid-1930s and gaining impetus in the 1950s, the poor increasingly settled in Suburbio, a fringe area west of downtown. Since the late 1970s there have been massive occupations of land by force, known locally as *invasiones*. The name also applies to the areas thus settled—generally, though not always, formerly unoccupied municipal land to the north and especially to the south of the city. Both Guasmo Norte and Guasmo Fertisa, discussed in chapter 3, were settled in this way. In recent years approximately 35 percent of Suburbio has been incorporated into the city proper via land titling and the provision of water and sewerage systems. The rest of this low-income fringe area remains unserviced and the occupants, who live in houses constructed of bamboo, are considered to be squatters. Roughly 58 percent of the popula-

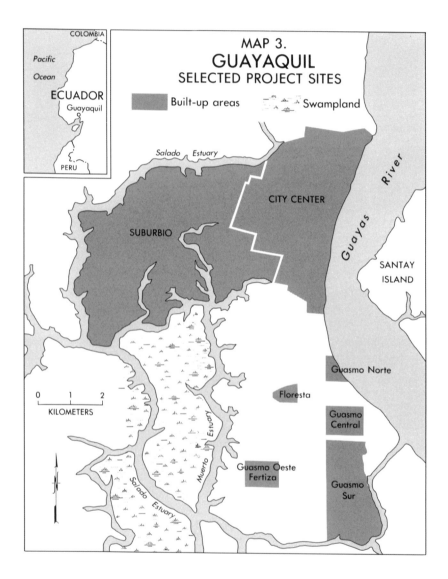

MAP 3.
GUAYAQUIL
SELECTED PROJECT SITES

Built-up areas   Swampland

COLOMBIA

Pacific

Ocean

ECUADOR
Guayaquil

PERU

Salado   Estuary

CITY CENTER

SUBURBIO

Guayas River

SANTAY
ISLAND

Guasmo Norte

Floresta

Guasmo
Central

0   1   2
KILOMETERS

Muerto Estuary

Guasmo Oeste
Fertiza

Guasmo
Sur

Salado Estuary

Table 2. Poorly Serviced Areas of Guayaquil, 1982

Area	Population (approximate)
Tugurios (inner city tenements)	200,000
Suburbio (partly legalized, mainly unserviced)	250,000
Squatter settlements	
Guasmo	200,000
Mapasingue and Prosperina	40,000
Los Cerros and Barrio Cuba	20,000
Total	710,000

Source: Jorge Salomón, "El Problema de la Vivienda en Guayaquil: Implicaciones y Soluciones" (Guayaquil, August 25, 1982), pp. 5, 6; Alfredo Rodríguez, "Notas para el Análisis del Suburbio y Tugurio de Guayaquil," *Revista Interamericana de Planificación*, vol. 19, no. 54 (June 1980), p. 146.

tion of Guayaquil now live in unsanitary, overcrowded conditions in tugurios or in the unserviced invasiones (see table 2).

The executing unit of the municipality of Guayaquil responsible for administering part of the World Bank loan estimated that the project would benefit close to 43 percent of this population of urban poor.[21] Although the World Bank made a more modest estimate of about half that amount, clearly the project was ambitious, multifaceted, and far-reaching in its intent.

As in La Paz, social and economic conditions in Guayaquil deteriorated during the fourteen-month period of my two stays there when income fell significantly behind inflation. From mid-1982 to mid-1983 median household income rose from 7,600 sucres to 10,700 sucres a month, an increase of 41 percent that was exceeded by a jump of 60 percent in the consumer price index in the same period.

Ecuador's weather contributed to its poor fortune. Because of the worst rains and floods in centuries it was calculated that in 1983 Ecuador would lose fully 32 percent of its agricultural production, a loss of more than $75 million.[22] As a result, food prices increased and food had to be imported. The problems in the countryside led, in turn, to increased migration to the cities.

About twenty minutes by bus from the center of the city is the new housing complex of Floresta (see map 4). Set off perhaps 200 meters from the main highway south to the new port of Guayaquil, it is one of three sites of the "Plan Roldos de Vivienda Popular." This plan was begun under the late President Jaime Roldos Aquilera and continued by his successor Osvaldo Hurtado to provide housing for the *marginados*—the poor traditionally excluded from the formal housing market.[23] The chief instruments

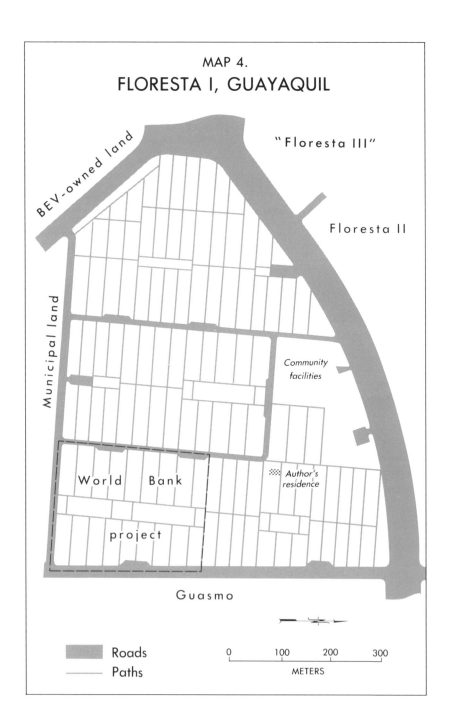

MAP 4.
FLORESTA I, GUAYAQUIL

BEV-owned land

"Floresta III"

Floresta II

Municipal land

Community
facilities

World   Bank

project

▓ Author's
residence

Guasmo

▓ Roads
— Paths

0   100   200   300
METERS

of the government housing policy are the National Housing Board (Junta Nacional de la Vivienda, or jnv), which is responsible for housing construction and policy, and the Ecuadorian Housing Bank (Banco Ecuatoriano de la Vivienda, or bev), which is responsible for housing finance. Floresta is the site of the original 558 houses built in 1979 as a pilot for the entire program by the National Housing Board. It is also the site of the World Bank–supported project (Floresta-birf) of 510 units, including 106 unfinished core houses. Floresta II houses another 900 families, all in core units built in late 1983. With the 1,612 units built by the private construction firm of Del Valle, Floresta has 3,580 houses, or 36 percent of the total 10,000 of the Plan Roldos in Guayaquil. These houses were built at a cost of roughly $4,000 each, about half the cost of the cheapest unit previously built by the Housing Bank in Guayaquil.

Floresta has the look of a typical government housing project: rows and rows of small houses built according to the same architectural plan. Yet, unlike many government projects, Floresta does not present a bleak image to the world. A walk down any one of the many footpaths that are its major arteries reveals that homeowners have individualized many if not most of the houses. They have added rooms, walls, new windows and doors, and, most striking to the foreign observer, have decorated windows with a vast assortment of iron grilles in ornate designs. It is characteristic of Floresta and the spirit of the people of Guayaquil that security has become the pretext for fanciful adornment.

Flowers of all types and colors and luxuriant tropical plants grow not only in small gardens in front of each house, but also in the strips between two footpaths. Constant daily care has been devoted to many of these small center strips, which are common property. The garden beds provide a lavish display of tropical flora bursting forth beside the hot cement walks. In viewing both the houses and gardens one feels there is something about this government project that the people like.

The relative value of housing is measured by its worth to its occupants. The previous residence is a major factor in a person's assessment of that worth. Visits that my local assistants and I made to the residences of a random sample of 54 of the 510 families who expected to move to Floresta-birf revealed the overwhelming significance of homeownership among the generally lower-middle-class families selected for this new housing project. What these future residents of the World Bank–supported sector of Floresta were to leave behind and what propelled them to move to this new site was not the squalor and misery of their original abodes. Most in fact lived in conditions that, for Guayaquil, were average or better than average. Rather, it was the desire to live in a house and on land that would someday be theirs.

All of the future residents of Floresta were renters. The dominant reason for moving to Floresta, stated by 60 percent of the sample, was to own a home. The next most frequently mentioned motives, greater comfort and a more pleasant environment, were given by only one-fifth of these persons. The future homeowners looked forward to having their monthly payments be an investment in their own property rather than a contribution to what they regarded as an alien landlord's ill-deserved affluence. They also wanted to have independence, often from other family members with whom they were then living. Most important, they needed to feel themselves masters of their own destiny, as symbolized by living in their own houses.

My own living experience in Floresta was far less comfortable than my residence in 8 de Diciembre in La Paz. I shared a house with a young couple and their baby (see figure 1). The house was cramped, stuffy, and hot. Other project residents complained of this as well, but in their case it may have been mitigated by pride of ownership and the ability to increase the size of their house and change internal spatial arrangements.[24] I was, however, able to enjoy the other two most often voiced qualities: the peace and quiet and the water and sewerage systems.

My house in Floresta was, like the majority of those around it, built by a private contractor. It was the last part of this area to be occupied, and other families were still arriving. When I arrived for my first stay of close to three months in early September 1982 only about half of the twenty-eight houses on both sides of the walkway that fronted my house were occupied. By mid-November of that year, all but four of these houses, or 86 percent, had families living in them. As can be seen from the plan of Floresta, map 4, my house was not far from the Floresta-BIRF area, which made it easy to visit there yet allowed me to keep a low profile.

Before moving in, I had the house painted inside and out, since the public housing units were turned over unpainted to occupants. My first few days and nights were among the most difficult I spent in Floresta, as illustrated by this excerpt from my diary:

La Floresta
Sunday, September 12, 1982

I have now been here for four nights, having arrived Wednesday, September 8. My impressions of life, of living conditions in La Floresta, are mixed but generally negative. I try to put myself in the place of those moving here from elsewhere, try to feel whatever advantage they do, but

Figure 1. Floor Plan for Author's Residence, Floresta, Guayaquil

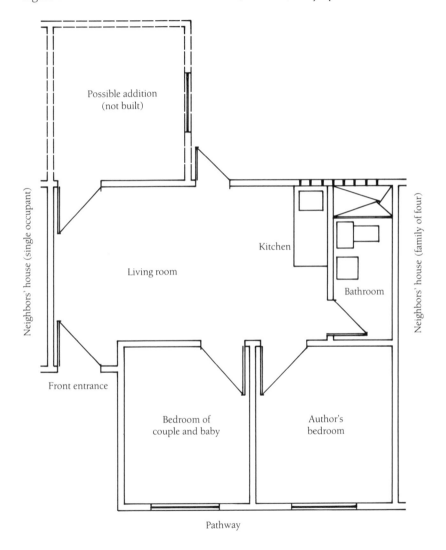

Possible addition
(not built)

Neighbors' house (single occupant)

Neighbors' house (family of four)

Kitchen

Living room

Bathroom

Front entrance

Bedroom of
couple and baby

Author's
bedroom

Pathway

I'm not at all sure they are comfortable or satisfied with conditions here either. We live in small, poorly ventilated cement cubicles, all in a row, amidst walkways of more cement. The heat, during at least 6 hours of the day, 11 to 5, is hardly bearable. Hard to understand the reasoning behind the architecture. The windows do not open, yet there is a screening above them for ventilation . . . To prevent the neighbors and passers-by from peering into one's house, people cover windows *and* screening with cloth "curtains" which block the little ventilation that exists.

Friday, 6:10 A.M., awakened by baby's crying, loud wails that seem to be in my own room—suddenly stopped and replaced by quick intermittent breathing of a small child being fed.

At first the walls seemed thinner on the side next to the family of four because of the noise. (The neighbor on the other side was not only farther removed but a lone guardian, awaiting his family, who arrived in mid-November.) But I soon discovered that the noise came from an open space of perhaps two inches between walls and ceiling. This was later closed up with cement by my neighbor, an act for which I was most grateful indeed. Although the negative impressions softened with time, the major cause of discomfort, the oppressive heat, remained a problem throughout my stay, alleviated somewhat by an electric fan. I only truly enjoyed this small house in Floresta either under the shower or very late at night when (generally) the heat had abated and a cooling breeze came through the screening, which I had left uncovered by curtains.

As might be expected in a public housing project, the people living in Floresta were more homogeneous and considerably better-off than residents of other low-income communities. Floresta households in July 1983 averaged annual earnings of 127,000 sucres, approximately the estimated median for Guayaquil at that time.[25] Data from the Housing Bank, taken from application forms (more reliable for demographic than for income data), revealed a younger and better educated group than my local assistants and I found among beneficiaries of the home improvement credit program of the Housing Bank. Heads of households in Floresta (among a group selected for the World Bank–supported Floresta-BIRF project) averaged thirty-five years of age as against forty-three for the home improvers. Of Floresta residents, 60 percent had completed primary school and 15 percent had completed secondary education, a dramatic contrast with the corresponding figures for the home improvers of 37 percent and 7 percent, respectively. Another key difference was that, to be eligible for the credit program, borrowers had to live in one of the inadequately serviced areas of

Guayaquil, while only 17 percent of the residents of Floresta came from these poor areas of the city.

Former living conditions of residents of Floresta were fair for about two-thirds and poor for the remaining third. The average number of rooms in the previous place of residence was 2.2, making for a relatively low internal density rate of 1.9 persons per room. More than two-thirds (69 percent) had had a private and independent kitchen, which their new houses in Floresta lacked. Almost two-thirds of the respondents had had their own running water (63 percent) and sanitary facilities (69 percent) in their previous residences.

Unemployment in Ecuador got markedly worse during my stay in Floresta. By mid-1983 persons in both neighboring houses and in my own were looking for work, because they had been laid off or were earning so little that a new source of income was necessary. Persons in their teens or early twenties who had little work experience were continually searching for employment but found no one willing to give them their first full-time job. Three young friends and neighbors, two with children, had despaired of finding work after months of searching. Another man living nearby who had been fully employed as a truck driver a year earlier now felt himself lucky to work as much as two days a week. Increasing numbers of unemployed and underemployed, especially young men, were seen standing idle in the streets of the city during normal work hours.

Not surprisingly, crime in this situation appeared to be on the rise. One frequent crime was robbery of bus passengers. A priest was assaulted in neighboring Guasmo to gain possession of a typewriter he was carrying. In one month four dogs on my pathway were killed. I did not understand why anyone would do this—until one morning my neighbor's water spigots were missing. The normal alarm had not been given by the barking of dogs. Then I knew why the dogs had been killed.

From the seven months I lived in each of the two low-income communities described here I gained a certain appreciation of what each group wanted from its respective project. Aside from the physical benefits of water, sewerage, wider streets (in 8 de Diciembre), or fully serviced housing in a calm setting (in Floresta), these groups were interested in gaining stature, in their own eyes and in the opinion of others as well. Much revolved around the concept of middle class, which in Latin America means something not so different from what it does in the United States: a comfortable house and the possibility of owning a car, living in respectable neighborhoods, getting a good education for one's children, and earning an income that allows a certain comfort and security.

In the United States, however, the majority of the population belongs to the middle class, whereas in Latin America generally no more than a third of the population does. It is much more difficult for upwardly mobile persons in La Paz or Guayaquil to acquire the highly prized symbols identifying them as middle class. The values that beneficiaries in 8 de Diciembre and Floresta ascribed to the urban projects must be understood in this light. In 8 de Diciembre the people who had signed contracts in the upgrading project wanted to gain entry into the ranks of the middle class through infrastructure provided by the project, which would place them in a "respectable" neighborhood. Most of the residents of Floresta, however, had already gained a foothold in the middle class. What they wanted was to consolidate their position through homeownership, to acquire not only their first significant capital good but also the freedom and status associated with owning a home of their own.

« **3** »

"OF COURSE WE COMMUNICATE"

According to the implementation schedule for the Guayaquil urban development project, construction for the upgrading of Guasmo Norte was to begin in the fourth quarter of 1980 and end in the first quarter of 1982. After nearly three years of discussion between community leaders and residents on one side and the implementing unit of the municipality on the other, however, the municipality canceled the proposed upgrading of Guasmo Norte. Instead, it decided to implement a similar project in a nearby settlement, Guasmo Fertisa. The primary reason given for this change was that the people of Guasmo Norte did not want the project while the people of Guasmo Fertisa apparently did.

The project plans for Guasmo Norte included piped water, landfill for streets, and individual ownership of plots. The improvements would have greatly increased the quality and quantity of water, made transportation cheaper and more convenient, and begun a land titling process to end the residents' squatter status and make them legal city residents. The monthly cost to each household for all these improvements would have been only about twice what the people were paying in 1979 for small quantities of unsanitary water brought in by trucks and unloaded into oil drums.

This is the story of why one low-income area of Guayaquil rejected a project offering seemingly obvious benefits, while another very similar area requested a project. To date neither area has been upgraded. A low-income area in La Paz, however, was successfully upgraded. The three areas taken together provide concrete lessons as to the value of the much-touted but seldom understood term, "communication." This and the following two chapters illustrate the kind of observations that, by providing a deep under-

standing of the community, can make a project more effective. Such observations are best made—and often can only be made—by the use of
participant observers and qualitative methods of inquiry.

Guasmo Norte

In 1975 an organized group of 400 families settled on a stretch of municipal
land in an area of southern Guayaquil called Guasmo. It was the first major
invasion by squatters in Guayaquil since 1972. Over the next three years,
four other groups, or *cooperativas*, moved into what came to be called
Guasmo Norte, until about 1,560 families—more than 9,000 persons—were
living in the area of 50.4 hectares.[1] These cooperativas have none of the
characteristics of cooperatives as known in Western Europe, the United
States, and many parts of Latin America. In Guayaquil they are formed
primarily for the purpose of obtaining land. After that, they ostensibly act as
intermediaries for the acquisition of land titles and infrastructure, but they
are becoming self-perpetuating political entities with little apparent man-
date or purpose.

By all accounts, including interviews with current residents who took part
in the invasion, the creation of a new community was an arduous process.
Before the marshy squatter site was habitable, the squatters had to clear
thickets of mangrove, a tough tropical tree, and haul in loads of crushed
rock for landfill.

The people of Guasmo Norte established their neighborhood when no
other groups were involved in similar endeavors and when city and
national authorities were opposed to such activity. In February 1976, in an
attempt to evict the squatters, national and local police raided the settlement and burned 260 houses to the ground. Most of the destroyed houses
belonged to members of Casitas del Guasmo, the first squatter cooperativa
to invade Guasmo.

The squatters refused to move, however, and the displaced families
returned several days after the burning. Although there were no additional
attempts at displacement, the five cooperatives banded together for their
common defense in an association known as the Front for the People's
Struggle (Frente de Lucha Popular). Their objective was to press authorities
for the right to remain where they were. They were assisted by the Faculty
of Architecture of the University of Guayaquil, which designed a site plan
for the settlement. The settlement evolved according to this plan into fairly
regular blocks of lots (9 × 22 meters), with an average low density of about

180 inhabitants per hectare and with ample open space, pedestrian walkways, and roads for vehicular traffic.

Had project officials been aware of this background, they should have realized that the community would probably be wary of collaborating with the authorities in the execution of a project. Indeed, this confrontational history would suggest the need for a major promotional campaign to win the confidence of not only the leaders, but also the rank and file of Guasmo Norte.

By the time of the decision to upgrade Guasmo Norte in late 1979, many additional settlers were moving into three other Guasmo areas, Centro, Sur, and Fertisa (west). Today the settled area of Guasmo covers 900 hectares with a population of nearly 200,000. Separated as it is from downtown Guayaquil by open land, some observers call Guasmo "the third city of Ecuador." Its growth was precipitous compared with the more than thirty years it took Suburbio to the west of Guayaquil to reach its population of roughly 350,000 on 1,510 hectares.

With few exceptions, the people of Guasmo are poor; their average household annual income in 1981 was roughly 165,000 sucres ($5,500).[2] President Jaime Roldos, elected in a return to civilian rule in 1979, was particularly concerned about the abject living conditions of the poor of Guayaquil, his native city. In his inaugural address, he mentioned Guasmo specifically and visited it during his first week in office.[3] Given the high profile of Guasmo, its obvious need for services, and the expressed concern of the president, Guasmo was a natural candidate for selection as an upgrading site.

Guasmo Norte was selected, however, before any discussion with community leaders or residents. Discussions began in early 1979 when two officials of the municipality's executing unit met with leaders of Guasmo Norte's cooperative organizations. The project was presented at a series of informal meetings, which included members of the community, the two municipal officials, and community leaders. As planned by the World Bank and the municipality it consisted of landfill for roads, electricity, legalization of land tenure, and a potable water system to be delivered by standpipes.

The question of standpipes figured prominently in the events leading to the community's eventual rejection of the upgrading project. In the discussions it became clear that the people of Guasmo Norte did not want standpipes. Three years later, at the time of my evaluation, the residents said that they had had negative experience with standpipes before coming to Guasmo Norte. They complained that everyone had to pay the same amount for the water even though some consumed far more than others, that dirty pools around the outlets presented a health hazard to children, that the pipes were often far away from the houses, that people had to wait in long lines, and that at night men would assault women coming for water.

In late 1979 the municipality changed the project design so that water would be piped directly to each house. This increased level of service was made possible when the National Chamber of Representatives decreed that the municipality should sell the land to the residents for 10 sucres per square meter rather than the 100 sucres per square meter originally planned. With the lower land costs, the people would be able to afford the more costly piped water; the project as a whole was to cost the residents no more than 550 sucres a month for fifteen years.

A second round of meetings was held in January and February 1980; first all the leaders met with municipal officials and then the major community associations—now six in number—met separately with the officials. At these meetings, according to municipal officials, the revised version of the project was presented and shown to include piped water with household connections.[4] The final meeting—in Casitas del Guasmo where the houses had burned three years earlier—dissolved into tumult. The agenda gave way to political harangues against the municipality, and rocks were thrown.

After the meetings, the executing unit gave the community associations time to consider the merits of the project and decide whether they wanted to participate or not. Despite the signs of resistance at Casitas del Guasmo, the municipal officials expected the community leaders to explain the project and help promote it. From my later discussions with leaders and other residents it seems certain that after the second round of meetings most of the leaders still did not want the project, regardless of what it proposed. At a meeting of municipality and community leaders in June, four months later, five of the six cooperatives rejected the project. There were subsequent negotiations with the one which wished to participate, Centro Cívico. But because of the very high per capita costs of bringing in off-site water pipes for a cooperative of only 335 families the municipality finally decided in early 1982 that there would be no upgrading in Guasmo Norte.

Although it is difficult to reconstruct the events and motivation that led to the rejection, there is little question that a failure of adequate communication between project officials and potential beneficiaries was at least partly responsible. The municipality's project preparation team had conducted a house-to-house survey in Guasmo Norte before the outset of the project, primarily to gather basic socioeconomic data such as family size, employment, and income. The project itself, however, was not mentioned at this early stage. On the basis of this survey, World Bank and local officials had decided that standpipes would be more affordable to the people than household connections. It now appears, from hindsight, that the question-naire survey method failed to elicit the people's negative attitude toward standpipes, their own criterion of affordability, or the opposition of their leaders, who may have played on the negative feelings of the people to undermine acceptance of the project. Qualitative interviews and open dis-cussions would very likely have revealed people's preferences and the political climate far better than did the preconstructed questionnaire.

From a survey I conducted as part of later qualitative research, it became clear that some community residents had never even heard about the project. They said they had not attended any meetings and had not been informed about the project by their leaders. About one-fifth (19 percent) of the sample of seventy-two households had no recollection of the project. Although the sample is too small (5 percent) to allow for reliable internal measures,[5] it is noteworthy that the cooperative with the least recollection was Casitas del Guasmo, which had had the turbulent meeting with offi-cials marked by anti-municipal speeches and demonstrations. Given the importance of drinking water to the suburban, nonserviced population, and the wide coverage of the meetings in the written record, it is somewhat surprising that so many people said they could not remember the project.[6]

Even more significant is the ignorance and misconceptions of most of the 81 percent that did remember the project. Of this group, twenty-four of the fifty-eight respondents could give no reason why the project had been rejected. Again, the greatest ignorance about what happened was in Casitas del Guasmo, where almost two-thirds of those who recalled the project could not explain why it was not executed. One reason given for the project's demise, mentioned as the principal reason by one-fifth of those who recalled it, was that it was a standpipe project, which the people did not want. This misconception is puzzling since the change to household connections in late 1979 had been discussed with all community leaders and at all the assemblies held in early 1980.[7]

Another principal reason for the project's rejection, given by a significant number of people (19 percent), was its high cost, a factor that indeed was a key issue during the deliberations.[8] Only two persons said the project was rejected because the people lacked confidence in the municipality. This finding is at odds with the municipality's own report, which judged the people's lack of confidence in the municipality to be the most important of nine reasons for the project's difficulties in Guasmo Norte. Most interesting and provocative was the response of four individuals that "the leaders were against it." The leaders indeed appeared to have played a most decisive role in the history of this project.

My first experience with the local leadership of Guasmo Norte convinced me that they were a key link between project and community, which had been poorly understood by the municipality. The leaders were articulate and respected, at least by some members of the community. But they seemed not only to have misunderstood the project but to have been most forceful in spreading this misunderstanding among their followers.

Before my first visit to Guasmo, where I had initially intended to live, I had been told many things about the place, none of them pleasant. Some taxi drivers would not go there at all. One municipal official, on hearing my plans, asked half seriously whether I had taken out life insurance. The women, I was told, carried razor blades in their mouths for defense, and knives were worn almost like items of apparel. On arriving, I found that as in so many poor city neighborhoods, what is said outside bears little relationship to what is going on inside: poor people trying to live their lives as best they can with what little they have. A family in Guasmo Norte—friends of neighbors of mine in Floresta—recommended that I see the president of their cooperative, Río Guayas, about the project: "He knows what happened; he was the one who was really involved with the project."

The president's house was made of bamboo, like most in Guasmo. When I arrived, he happened to be meeting with some residents of the cooperative to discuss a water project. There were perhaps twenty people—more women than men, as often seems to be the case at neighborhood meetings in Guayaquil—seated in the large, poorly lit room with a breeze coming through the bamboo slats. After I explained that I was curious about the water and landfill project in Guasmo Norte that never got started, there was a stillness in the room.

The host and president then brought me a map of a water project for Guasmo Norte for which he and other leaders "were going to get 50 percent funding from the government." The other 50 percent the people would pay for. That seemed an interesting idea, but I was still curious about that other water and landfill project. What happened to it? The man began to explain, in somewhat faltering fashion, at which point a strong, educated voice said from the other side of the room, "The project was rejected for two reasons: first, it was too expensive and, second and most important, it was a stand-pipe project and we have found from experience that standpipes are not good." This was a surprise to me because I felt sure from conversations with the municipality and the World Bank that water was to have been connected to households. Not wanting to argue with these leaders, especially in front of their constituents, I feigned confusion. They then took me to a similar meeting in 25 de Enero, another of the five original cooperatives, where the articulate, nonresident leader reiterated that the people there did not like standpipes either, especially expensive ones. "But if the project had been household connections and at a reasonable cost, of course we would accept it, wouldn't we?" The assembled blank faces said in a muffled chorus, "Yes, of course."

The people of Guasmo Norte were by the time of my evaluation, in late 1982, paying roughly 550 sucres a month for an average of twenty-five tanks of often contaminated water, or about what they would have been paying for a far greater supply of clean water piped into their houses, had they accepted the upgrading project. Many still lived over brackish, unsanitary water and most of the roads remained unfilled—dusty in the summer, muddy in the winter. The people of Guasmo Norte needed landfill, appeared anxious to have a constant supply of good drinking water, and were clearly willing to pay for both.

I concluded from survey data and discussions held in Guasmo Norte and elsewhere in Guayaquil that most of the local leadership did not want to collaborate with the municipality and thus did not promote, but rather subverted, this upgrading project. This was stated point-blank in four of the five individual interviews I had with leaders in Guasmo Norte. Only one cooperative, Centro Cívico, had held meetings with the municipality implementing unit at the block level rather than at the level of the overall cooperative. Significantly, Centro Cívico was the one cooperative that accepted the project. Municipality representatives never discussed the project with individual residents in their homes. In the Los Vergeles cooperative there had been no meeting at all about the project because, one municipal spokesman said, "there was a confusion of leadership there." From in-depth discussions with the titular leader of this association, who had been sympathetic to the project, and with other residents of this area, it appeared that this confusion had been engineered by leaders of other cooperatives who were opposed to the project.

Part of the problem of communication lay in the weakness of the implementing institution. The project was the municipality's first upgrading experience. The implementing unit was seriously understaffed, especially in the social division, which consisted of one person throughout these arduous events. The unit was working with insufficient autonomy in a municipal administration that apparently gave it little support and eventually lost legitimacy itself. The mayor of Guayaquil was impeached and imprisoned (on charges unrelated to the project) in mid-1981, and this had a traumatic, nearly paralytic effect on all municipal work for some time. Furthermore, the implementing unit received little guidance in the social area from the World Bank, which at the time of project preparation was itself still in an exploratory phase of its work in the urban sector.

The sociopolitical dynamics of a community are as important to understand as the technical aspects and design of any upgrading project. This is especially true in poor countries such as Ecuador, where people in urban settlements are united by a common need for improvements in their living conditions. These improvements become the carrots used by populist parties to win votes. Politicians work through barrio organizations or, in squatter settlements such as Guasmo Norte, through cooperatives or precooperatives. These associations are sometimes converted directly into electoral committees to drum up votes for a party during election campaigns. It is at this time that the people see the most, and sometimes the only, physical improvements in their residential area; some of these improvements stop, uncompleted, on election day.

Land tenure, which the World Bank had singled out as without doubt the most difficult aspect of this project, was a point of contention in Guasmo Norte.[9] Political rivalry between Guayaquil and the party of the Roldos government created an adversarial climate in which the central government was unwilling to help the municipality resolve the land issue. Land, like water, sewerage systems, and street paving, cannot be acquired by poor people except through the cooperation of a governmental authority. These items thus become subject to political brokering at all levels, from the presidency of the nation to the precooperative of the poorest urban squatter settlement.[10]

The implementation unit of the municipality and World Bank staff did not understand the nature of the local leadership in Guasmo Norte. Most of the leaders of Guasmo Norte were directly or indirectly tied to the Movimiento Popular Democrático, a radical leftist party extremely critical of the central government. Under the best of circumstances, it would have been unusual for persons of this political persuasion to have readily served as promoters and channels of communication for a project administered by the municipality. In this case, distrust had been aroused by past attempts of the municipality, albeit under a different mayor, to eradicate the community by burning its houses. Although one might question why an area marked by such conflict had been selected for upgrading, once the selection was made it clearly called for a far more probing analysis of the situation and more extensive communication and promotion throughout the community than was achieved here.

Guasmo Fertisa

Guasmo Fertisa—so named because it is adjacent to a large fertilizer company, FERTISA—with a population of about 25,000, actively petitioned the municipality in early 1982 to install a water system with household connections. My observations and surveys there revealed an interplay of politics and economics that contrasted sharply with the events in Guasmo Norte. My team of local researchers and I were interested in finding out what accounted for the difference in attitude and whether the settlement's leaders were accurately representing the wishes of the general population in petitioning for an upgrading project. Since the request stated that the people were willing to pay for the household connections, we sought to determine how much residents were actually willing to pay.

In November 1982, several months after the residents' request for the upgrading project, we conducted a brief survey of a 3 percent sample, or 145 families, of the 4,850 families organized in five cooperatives. The residents of Guasmo Fertisa's sixth cooperative, with 45 families, did not participate in the survey because they feared they would be forced to move to make way for essential public works and were apprehensive about outsiders.

One reason for the willingness of Guasmo Fertisa's leaders to collaborate with the government in 1982 was the help given in their earlier struggle to claim the land and build new homes. Although there had been some government resistance to the invasion when it began in 1978, it was replaced by significant support from the party that was coming to national power at that time. This party, the Concentración de Fuerzas Populares (CFP), and the late President Roldos helped Guasmo Fertisa by supplying it with most of its landfill as well as by protecting the community from eviction. It is no accident that five of the six cooperatives of Fertisa are named after the first leader of the CFP and the relatives of the late President Roldos.

In addition, there were in Guasmo Fertisa middle-class leaders striving for the increased land values and status that upgrading would have brought the area. This "bourgeois" upward mobility was very reminiscent of 8 de Diciembre in La Paz. It was particularly true of the president of one of the Fertisa cooperatives, a lawyer who sparked the desire for this project, promoting it among the other leaders and among his own cooperative members, contacting the municipality, and even sending a telegram to the head of urban projects for Latin America at the World Bank. This kind of leadership, which is motivated by middle-class values, will cooperate with government authorities, but its orientation is more private than political; it does not see infrastructure or land as appropriate items to barter for political support. In the lawyer's words, "water has no political color."

On the question of the amount residents were willing to pay monthly for the water hookups, our results differed from the assumptions of the project planners up to that point. Clearly, the issues raised by the attempt to pipe in water to low-income families look different from the perspective of the families themselves. The municipal executing unit had calculated that a monthly payment of 550 sucres per family for five years would pay the cost of the project in Guasmo Fertisa; this figure was based on rule-of-thumb estimates of affordability from overall income figures rather than on people's stated preferences. Since the figure was no more than residents of Fertisa were already paying for trucked-in water, the municipality had assumed they would be willing to pay at least as much for more and better water supplies.

My survey showed a much more complex picture. Almost all (97 percent) of the residents of Guasmo Fertisa wanted the water project for their area and were willing to pay for it, although generally at somewhat lower monthly rates. (The five persons who were not in favor of the project either thought they should be provided water free or did not trust the municipality.) People were unwilling to pay as much for better and more water as they were paying for water from trucks. They said they feared an overcommitment to monthly charges when their employment and income were unstable. The amount a household would pay for water was found in the survey to be directly related to its income, as it is for other goods.[11] As would be expected, it was this overall level of earnings, more than the proportion of family income spent on water, that influenced the level of payments chosen by each family. Most important, a majority of the people of Guasmo Fertisa were reluctant to enter into obligations requiring monthly payments of more than a nominal amount.[12] The families willing to meet the pre-established monthly rate of 550 sucres were paying about 7.9 percent of their income for water from trucks at the time of the survey. Those who felt 550 sucres was too much, however, were already paying 12 percent of their income for water from trucks—but they were willing to pay only 315 sucres for piped water, or little over half the pre-established figure and a mere 6 percent of their average income. This reluctance to pay for piped water even the amount they were paying to the trucks appears to be rooted in the condition of poverty itself.

As in certain other cities of Latin America (I recall Port-au-Prince, Haiti, in particular) the poor in Guayaquil paid far more for water hauled in by truck than the higher-income families paid for water via household connections. This difference was estimated at 800 percent in 1976.[13] More than two-thirds (68 percent) of the households covered in our sample had monthly family earnings of 6,500 sucres ($112) or less, of whom almost half (38 percent) earned less than the 4,500-sucre ($78) minimum wage. Many of these very poor families have many children for whom water is essential for drinking, bathing, and washing of clothes. Yet they are among the mass of underemployed who do not receive fixed salaries and have incomes that may vary widely.

I interviewed one woman by her one-room bamboo shack as she was bathing one small child, while four others, none over eight or nine years old, played nearby. She felt that a piped-in water supply would be a definite improvement over the trucked water she was buying. With all the dish-washing and bathing of children and the unreliable truck delivery, water often ran out. When asked how much she was willing to pay each month for a piped-in water supply she called over a neighbor and they figured they could afford about 300 sucres per household, or about half of what the municipality had estimated they would need to pay for five years to cover the cost of both water and installing the system. Yet these two households paid more than twice that amount monthly for one or sometimes two barrels of water a day from trucks. When I mentioned this disparity one of them answered: "If we can't meet a monthly payment the municipality will cut us off from the system until we pay what we owe. My husband works as a bricklayer; sometimes there is no work. Usually we have the 20 sucres to buy a barrel of water, and if we don't we can borrow a little from a neighbor until the next day. But a payment of 550 sucres each month is too much for poor people like us." Low income is thus accompanied by a fear of falling into debt because of inability to meet monthly payments and then of being cut off from all water.

As with many project components which appear so advantageous that they need little promotion or explanation, a piped-in water system presents certain problems not readily visible from outside the community of poten-tial users. The foremost problem is the obligation of low-income persons to meet monthly water payments of approximately 10 percent of household income—a far larger percentage than for middle- and upper-income families and a heavy burden. The compensating factors of better quality, greater supply, and (over time if not immediately) reduced expenses may seem self-evident to someone looking at the purely technical or economic aspects of water supply. But they are far less important to a population not accus-tomed to having water piped into their homes, yet very conscious of day-to-day expenditures and reluctant to incur obligations that would be difficult to meet.

It is necessary first to understand the concerns of the beneficiaries or consumers, then to alleviate them, if possible, by sound project design (based in part on these concerns), and then to promote acceptance. Negotiations would have allowed monthly water charges to be set at a level that would have alleviated people's apprehensions and would thus have been accepted. Such negotiations are most easily done via the local leaders. Where the leadership favors the project, as in Guasmo Fertisa, the chance of success is far greater than where leaders are opposed, as was the case in Guasmo Norte. In all cases, the people of a community need to be seen as a group distinct from and not always well represented by their own leadership. Understanding, communication, and promotion are needed at both levels.

8 de Diciembre

In an area of La Paz that was once open fields and then shacks along alleyways crisscrossing the side of a hill, a pleasant urban neighborhood is being formed, thanks in good part to the upgrading project. The June 10, 1979, agreement between the municipality of La Paz and the 8 de Diciembre Neighborhood Committee stated that the project executing unit, HAM-BIRF, would be committed to "the execution of the works of construction of sewerage and drainage systems, the installation of drinking water, the construction of curbs and sidewalks and the approval of a plan of urbanization, including street widening, for which the community was obliged to pay the costs and to supply communal labor on the days and dates to be indicated."

The community had been given three improvement options, all containing water and sewerage. The first option included nothing more, the second included sidewalks as well, and the third sidewalks and street paving. The community chose the second option, which would cost each participating household 80.51 pesos ($3.66) per square meter, or 222 pesos ($9.06) a month for fifteen years for a plot of 200 square meters. Two hundred and twenty families signed up for the project, all but nine of the property holders in the project area, the central part of 8 de Diciembre.[14] Project work on street widening began December 10, 1979.

From April 24 to May 3, 1982, my two local assistants and I conducted in-depth interviews with representatives of twenty-five households selected at random from the project area. We talked to each family at least two and often three times so as to gain their confidence and increase our under-

standing of them. All but four persons interviewed had entered into contracts with the project; of the four, three were renters and one was of the
small minority that had refused to sign up for the project.

In the interviews the final questions revolved around whether, after more
than two years of project life, the resident was satisfied with the project.
Despite the obvious benefits—widened streets and a sewerage system—
already received by the families in the project area, only a bare majority,
fourteen persons, expressed satisfaction with the project; eight of the
twenty-five interviewed were not satisfied, and the remaining three were
indifferent. Typical of the critical comments was the statement by one
community leader: "The concept of this project is very good. But the
execution has had problems. This project should have been finished last
year. It is our money that is paying for this. The people working on the
project [HAM-BIRF] are too distant from us. We should have water by now.
Many families still don't have any access to sewerage pipes." Additional
evidence of dissatisfaction was the fact that as of April 1983, after slightly
more than three years of project execution, roughly half (52 percent) of the
beneficiary households were behind on their monthly payments by an
average of four months.[15]

A year later, a repeat survey of a larger sample of thirty-three households
(15 percent of all households in the project area) found the degree of
satisfaction with the project on the rise; almost three-quarters (73 percent)
of those interviewed expressed approval. A considerable number of people
were still not satisfied, however, with a project that had significantly
improved their living conditions and is considered by World Bank staff to
be one of the best Bank-supported upgrading projects anywhere in the
world. I attribute this negative attitude, at least in part, to insufficient or
improper communication between implementing agency and beneficiaries.
Three aspects of this project illustrate how faulty communication can
reduce people's appreciation for and participation in what is otherwise an
excellent urban development project.

Delay

Delay is as much a perceived as an actual phenomenon. In 8 de Diciembre
the people attributed delays to the indifference or purposeful neglect of
municipal authorities. In fact, much of the delay was caused by factors over
which implementation staff had no control. The manner in which the
community was informed about delay, however, the number of times executing unit personnel gave target dates of completion which were not met,

and the close to absolute lack of any explanation of the cause of delay exacerbated the problem. These problems of communication transformed delay into one of the principal factors undermining the people's trust in project implementation staff.

The invitation to the ceremony of the signing of the agreement between the municipality and the Neighborhood Committee on June 10, 1979, stated that the project would be completed in fourteen months. At that rate, it would have been finished by March 1981. But because of a number of delays in execution, the project was formally declared finished on December 8, 1982; in other words, it took two and one-half times longer than intended. This kind of project delay, though exceeding the norm, is not unusual. In a World Bank comprehensive review of urban development projects worldwide it was stated that "implementation of the average Bank project (5.4 years) requires 40 percent more time than originally estimated (3.8 years)."[16]

Project administrators could have explained much of the delay to the satisfaction of community residents. With three changes of government in the first two years of project execution and widespread allegations of corruption elsewhere in the government, the delay could easily have been attributed, at least in part, to the unstable political climate of Bolivia. Another cause of delay was the excessively bureaucratic procedures for obtaining approval of various project components. Bolivia's extremely cumbersome procurement regulations require many agencies to sign off, often even the president's office. In one notable case involving permission for a water system in one of the upgrading sites in El Alto, approval of a contract took more than a year from the time the technical decision was made by the implementation unit.

The biggest problem, however, was that the community was given wrong information or none. The slowness of project execution was readily understandable and did not unduly bother local project staff, but it seemed ominous to project beneficiaries.

Clear Delineation of Responsibilities

A good deal of friction between the residents of 8 de Diciembre and the implementation unit could have been avoided if it had been clearer who was expected to do what. Many families believed that upgrading was to include a number of improvements that were in fact not part of the project agreement; they also thought that all improvements were to be done by the implementation unit, perhaps in association with the Neighborhood Committee, but not by the residents themselves. The misunderstanding was only partially due to faulty execution of the project. It was as much or more a result of inadequate communication by the implementation unit, which in turn led to the beneficiaries' perception that the project had shortcomings.

Much of this problem of perception became clear to me in February 1983 on my return to 8 de Diciembre after an absence of eight months. During my absence the project had officially ended and all the work had been completed: streets had been widened and water connections and sewerage lines had been installed. Yet many residents believed that the project was not really complete, that there was unfinished business which the project had failed to address. The street lighting was still inadequate, the dirty and unruly Cotahuma River had still not been completely channeled, streets were left unpaved, sidewalks were cobblestoned but not finished in cement, there was no community center, and so on. None of the missing improvements, however, was part of the World Bank's agreement with the municipality.

Another problem was that after more than three years of experience in an upgrading project, less than a third (30 percent) of the sample of thirty-three families interviewed mentioned themselves as the agent of change that should resolve the deficiencies. Another third were of the opinion that the Neighborhood Committee was the key agent for area improvements. Well over a third (39 percent) of the respondents felt that the solution to area needs lay entirely outside the neighborhood of 8 de Diciembre, either with the project executing unit (30 percent) or the municipality (9 percent). The people of 8 de Diciembre still perceived themselves to be the object of an upgrading effort. For the most part they considered themselves to be passive recipients of physical products, and they were waiting for their own leadership or outside forces to guide and manage the improvement of their own neighborhood.

The first communication problem (delineating what the project was and was not) was less far-reaching than the second (transmitting a clear message that much of the improvement work was up to the people themselves). Project personnel contributed to the first problem by making commitments they were not in a position to fulfill regarding street lighting and the channeling of the river. These elements depended on other city agencies, and HAM-BIRF commendably attempted to pressure them to gain the additional improvements. However, if HAM-BIRF had been more explicit with the beneficiaries about what they could and could not reasonably expect of the project, a major cause of dissatisfaction would have been reduced.

Nevertheless, there is perhaps a natural tendency for people to expect more of an improvement project than it is intended to provide. The common attitude was, "This project was supposed to improve this entire neighborhood. Until that river is channeled (or the streets are lighted or paved, or a community center is built, or some other goal is attained), this project hasn't done all it should have." To some degree these sentiments may be inevitable, good communication notwithstanding. People look at improvements in their communities in a more holistic fashion than project designers and implementors who must be concerned with the financing and execution of individual components.

The confusion regarding degree and kind of community participation was cause for greater concern. At a meeting of the Neighborhood Committee just before the end of my first stay the topic of community participation came up. Several of the officers said it had never been clear to them just what role the community, committee, or residents were supposed to have in the improvement process. The project executing unit had expected that several improvements, such as paving the streets and building a community center, would get done by community efforts. Yet it had failed to communicate just how the community was to organize itself to do this. In part this was because it had wrongly assumed that the community was a functioning unit ready to work on its own self-improvement.

In more than two years only four of the twelve streets were paved, three of which were among the shortest and narrowest of the barrio. Land donated to the community of 8 de Diciembre in mid-1982 as a site for a community center remained vacant as late as February 1984, my final visit to La Paz. Although the families who lived in 8 de Diciembre did have certain common needs, they had not worked on these improvements because they were not a cohesive community and did not have a tradition of working as a unit to solve those needs. Rather, 8 de Diciembre, like many spontaneous urban settlements, was made up of many small cliques of friends, relatives, and isolated families of diverse social and economic backgrounds. Before effective communication could take place the atomistic nature of this settlement needed to be understood. If the project staff had realized how loose or nonexistent were the ties between the households of the area, measures could have been devised to bring the people together to solve common needs.

Technical Matters

During the first year of project execution one of the residents complained to a project official that the quality of pipe being installed for the sewerage system was poor and would deteriorate rapidly during the heavy rainy season. The official, who had been trained as an engineer, replied that this man, who was not an engineer, did not know what he was talking about. Now irate, the man proceeded to carry his complaint and a piece of the controversial pipe to the director of the municipality's pipe-making division. There, the resident's judgment was confirmed. As a result, much of the piping in 8 de Diciembre was replaced with better material. This outspoken individual, a self-made man of considerable means, became the project's most severe critic. Largely as a result of this stance, he was later elected president of the Neighborhood Committee.

During the execution of the project in 8 de Diciembre other technical problems arose that were not as dramatic as the incident of the pipe but ended less auspiciously for the community: ditches dug for sewer pipes were left open for seven months; piping was put too close to the street surface (according to many residents) for an easy gravitational flow from houses to the main line; and no water or sewer pipes were laid to serve the fifteen or so families who lived along the river bed. Generally, personnel from the implementation unit were able to give good reasons for each situation. Yet the people affected were seldom made to understand these reasons to their satisfaction.

The potential for poor communication between project implementation personnel and community residents is great. One is middle class, the other generally poor; one is professional, the other most often untrained beyond primary school; one is an outsider, the other lives in the area being affected by the project. Often, the poorest residents in an area will be the last to make their voices heard—out of fear or insecurity, or perhaps because of the many times their opinions went unheard even when they had been expressed. It is a mistake to assume, however, that because poor people say less they are more content. When an official from the implementing unit said that the only critics of the project were the four or five people in the community who knew how to read he revealed how little he understood the reasons behind the silence of many low-income persons. For good communication to occur, there must be someone who listens. If the person affected by a development project is reluctant to speak, it is incumbent on project personnel to encourage self-expression so that communication does take place and professional outsiders and residents can work together.

Lessons

There is often an assumption among development professionals that a good development project sells itself. The project is seen to have a viability apart from the people for whom it is intended. Perhaps the main lesson underlying the stories told here is that to be successful a project should be designed and executed with significant participation of the beneficiaries at each step of the way. Beneficiaries participate when they understand and appreciate how a project may help them. Project designers create helpful projects when they understand the needs and priorities of the people for whom help is intended. Effective understanding of these people is achieved by listening to them. This understanding is the basis for the kind of communication between people and managers which underlies both the participation of the community and the success of the project.

Only from the perspective of individuals being subjected to a development project is it possible to see just how wide is the gap separating them from the architects and managers of the project. Why was a project designed to include public standpipes for water when the recipients had such an adverse reaction to them? When design standards were raised to include domestic water connections, why did many community residents fail to learn that the change had been made? Why did an executing unit believe that by relating to the community leadership they were at the same time relating to the people of the community, when in fact there were major differences of interest between the leaders and the people they were supposed to represent? Why was the significance of the political leanings of local leadership underestimated by both World Bank and project implementation unit officials? Why did another implementing unit assume that through community participation roads would be paved and a community center built when the people of the community had never worked together on any major undertaking as a collective unit? Why did the project unit fail to communicate effectively the reasons for project delays? The answer to all of these questions is that project planners and implementors had an incomplete perception of the people and were blinded to important aspects of the reality they were trying to change.

The problems of communication addressed in this chapter do not arise from any lack of professional competence of the project staff. Rather, these problems are endemic to the nature of development work itself when people of very diverse status and experience attempt to work together without first establishing the common ground necessary for mutual understanding and dialogue. The development professional must adapt his technical expertise to the values and beliefs of the people who are the subjects of development. This adaptation is based on understanding the people on their own terms.

The communication between project staff and the residents of Guasmo Norte which preceded and initiated the upgrading project was misleading to both parties because it was based on insufficient understanding. How does one know what kind of local leadership exists in a community? How may one become familiar with individuals' preferences and values with regard to such technical matters as standpipes for water? And how may one gain understanding of the meaning of monthly payments to a person earning a low and unstable income? The answer to these and other questions and a basic determinant of a project's success is to learn to listen to the people as they tell their stories, recount their experiences, and express their feelings about issues which matter both to them and to the project.

Understanding, communication, participation—these basic words of human intercourse are vital to any successful development activity. All have been shown to be a function of the relationship between project professionals and the people, or beneficiaries. This relationship is generally weak, however, in large part because of the difference in perspective between the two groups. People and planners need to come closer together. Managers must learn to reach out more effectively into the communities where they want their projects to work. At the same time, they must help build up the community so that it may better make itself heard.

Development planners and managers need to develop their antennae, to extend their eyes and ears into the communities where they are planning and carrying out projects. The first need is for the developmentalist to spend time with the people, not in his role as a professional but as a person. The most successful managers in private business have understood and acted for years on this principle of proximity to both customers and workers.[17] Yet no professional project manager has the time needed for the kind of understanding and communication called for here, and few staff persons in development organizations are trained and encouraged to be the needed eyes and ears among the beneficiaries. To develop effective outreach into communities a cadre of both staff and consultants must be formed to learn the needs and wants of the potential or actual beneficiaries, to feed back accurate perceptions to the planners and managers, and then to help the beneficiaries understand the nature of the project and their role in it as it is being executed.

These functions often fit within the job description of the social staff, but social workers tend to spend more time in their offices than with the low-income beneficiaries and are not familiar with the technical aspects of the project, which are often the matters that concern the beneficiaries the most. Typically, there is a sharp dichotomy between technical and social staff: the technician works on what is important to the people but does not listen or talk to them, while the social worker, the only one who does talk to the people, is ignorant of technical matters and seldom communicates with technical staff. Staff in the field need greater integration, so that diverse specialists work more closely together and each can at least explain the work of the other; all should be able and willing to communicate effectively with beneficiaries.

For good communication to take place, the community must be sufficiently organized and confident to speak on its own behalf. The new low-cost housing project of Floresta is a good example of an area lacking both effective outreach and community organization. The Ecuadorian Housing Bank, the project implementing agency, did not send any representative to the community meetings during the ten-month period of my association with the project. Nor did it exert any efforts to organize the community.

While living in Floresta I sensed a lack of community organization. The residents of this housing project had a legitimate desire and need for effective channels through which they could constructively voice their opinions regarding the improvements in their community. Yet the Housing Bank had no program to foster community organization. It was almost like selecting a man, a woman, and children at random from a crowd, placing them in a house, and expecting them to act as a family.

Floresta-BIRF, the unit of the Housing Bank implementing the World Bank project, had planned for community organization before people moved into their new housing, but they made the mistake of organizing on the basis of blocks. Once in Floresta, residents tended to socialize with each other along the pathways at their front door, rather than with others in their block (most of whom lived in houses facing other walkways). Hence, the organization by block broke down. No new organization was done by walkway. After two months of residence only three of the twenty walkways held meetings.

According to our survey, 71 percent of the residents of Floresta knew their elected representative, but less than a third felt this person was helping to improve the area. Only 36 percent of Floresta residents sampled went to meetings with their walkway neighbors, most often because no meetings were held. Many others did not attend meetings because they felt little would be accomplished by doing so.

An example of the low level of community organization may be seen in the issue of transportation. By far the largest number of people interviewed felt inadequate transportation to be Floresta's worst problem. A petition requesting another bus line for Floresta was circulated among residents and was to be sent to the president of the transportation commission of Guayas, the state in which Guayaquil is located. I joined the two neighbors who had initiated the petition and remember the response of one man whose signature we requested: "I am on the central council for Floresta and this should properly have come from us." At first this man refused to sign on these grounds; later in the conversation he did sign, saying it was a good idea even though it had not come through the council. Later an open letter from the presidents of the three Plan Roldos housing complexes, including Floresta, was printed in the leading newspaper of Guayaquil, *El Universo* (July 21, 1983). The letter complained about uncertainty over the price of the houses, poor garbage collection, and bad road maintenance but said nothing about inadequate transport. The residents of my walkway had not been informed of the contents of the letter, and this caused a major falling out between various residents and the elected representative. Clearly, communication was moving neither up nor down within the formal community organization, on this as on many other issues.

Effective community organization should encourage a dialogue between residents and a housing institution. When, as in Floresta, the housing agency administers the project for the first few years of its life, this dialogue is the chief political instrument the residents have for improving their living area. Although some management theorists worry that community organization may threaten the existing institutional order, in Floresta it was the absence of organization and constructive dialogue that led the residents to seek redress for their grievances via publicity in the press and petitions to politicians.

In addition, an organized community can administer its own needs far better than an unorganized one. A few weekends of concerted communal effort cleaned up the walkway where I lived and several others in Floresta; they then looked much better than the majority of walkways, where internal organization was less tight. In another joint effort residents installed lights for the pathway and increased security.

Community organization was also needed in 8 de Diciembre in La Paz. HAM-BIRF recognized its value and actively and successfully organized other upgrading areas by forming small work groups on each street to carry out self-help activities that complemented the project improvements. Another need in 8 de Diciembre was to correct the imbalance between the technical staff and the community and ensure that they both had equal influence. One idea that came out of discussions with community residents was for the community to hire its own technical experts as a professional counterpart to the executing agency in reviewing cost figures for bids and contracts and assessing the quality of project execution.

The British have a system whereby the contractor seeks the counsel of an independent assessor to confirm or revise the plans and designs of a builder or architect. In the United States advocate planners sometimes perform a role similar to that envisaged here. What my neighbors in 8 de Diciembre wanted was a professional entity that spoke for and was responsible to the community—a core of professionals who would work part-time, probably no more than a few days a month, and thus keep costs to the community low. The creation of professional units accountable directly to low-income communities warrants consideration. These "people's professionals" could help ensure better execution of the project, better response to community needs, better communication between community and executing agency, and ultimately greater satisfaction on the part of community residents.

La Paz

View of La Paz from the Zona Alta, with 8 de Diciembre in the foreground.

Calle R. Gutierrez, the main street of 8 de Diciembre. The pile of rocks for paving the street was left untouched for several months.

The author's one-room residence in 8 de Diciembre, originally intended as a shop.

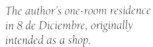

La Paz (continued)

Calle 2 (Second Street), where the author lived in 8 de Diciembre, is the road going up the hill to the left.

An unchanneled stretch of the Cotahuma River.

The channeled section of the Cotahuma River.

Guayaquil

Neighbors improving the center strip of a pathway in Floresta. The author's house is the second from the right.

Finished and unfinished piso-techo houses in Floresta.

The border area between Floresta (right) and Guasmo (background), with garbage from Guasmo dumped in the foreground.

Guayaquil (continued)

A piso-techo home that is being improved by the owner.

The back yards of Floresta. Houses in the background have been enlarged by the addition of upper stories or an extra room on the back.

The unused health clinic in Floresta.

« **4** »

CATALYTIC EFFECTS OF DEVELOPMENT

Development is a process that induces people to change their lives for the better. To be effective, a development project must enlist the cooperation of the people, who become the agents of their own improvement. One gauge of a project's success is the degree to which it has encouraged people to do things for themselves beyond what the project did for them. This encouragement of the people to act on their own behalf may be seen as the catalytic effect of a development project.

Various components in the two urban projects in Guayaquil and La Paz had this catalytic effect. The promotion of self-improvement was either direct (credit to artisans or for home improvement) or indirect (additions to the houses and rental income generated by the provision of urban infrastructure). The catalytic effect was most apparent at the individual or household level; at the community level self-help was more a goal than a reality. When people were encouraged to continue an ongoing process of improving their home or small business, they were more responsive than in the case of something started by others and provided to them as part of the project, such as incomplete, core housing.

Upgrading

When I returned to La Paz for my second stay after an absence of eight months, the neighborhood of 8 de Diciembre looked at first glance much as I remembered it from the previous year. Most of the streets were still unpaved; the Cotahuma River remained a garbage-strewn, foul-smelling stream as before; the community center was still unbuilt. Yet there had been changes, not in the common areas but in the houses and individual plots of land. From a quick visual survey, it appeared that well over half of the houses were undergoing some major physical improvement, such as the construction of a wall to enclose the yard and the addition of a second story to the house.

The room where I had lived was much as I had left it, but there, too, some changes had taken place. The owners had placed a light over the entrance and installed a showerhead in the cement-floored free-standing bathroom, which I shared with the landlord's family. A cement patio now covered what had been a large patch of bare dirt in front of the bathroom door. Since the street had no public lighting, the light over the door was a welcome addition. Even more important was the shower, which shortened my early-morning sponge bath with boiled water from a plastic basin. And the patio made for less muddy feet, although the road beyond the wall bordering my landlord's land was still unpaved dirt.

My general impression of 8 de Diciembre, after I had been back for a few weeks, was that the area continued to undergo significant improvement, but mainly of private property belonging to landowners who had signed up for the project. The public amenities of an improved urban neighborhood—paved streets, lighting, communal meeting space, health and recreational facilities—were still very much absent. Subsequent trips revealed that some of these improvements were eventually made. The World Bank's investment in physical infrastructure, water sewerage, and street widening had initiated a process of self-help that in less than three years led to many home improvements and eventually to general upgrading of the community as well.[1]

My assistants and I conducted intensive qualitative interviews with about 15 percent of the 220 beneficiary households in April 1982 and again in April 1983, more than two and three years after the project had begun in December 1979. Each sample was randomly selected and distinct from the other. Households were selected by assigning a number to each house on a project map of the area, writing each number on a separate piece of paper, tossing the pieces in a hat, and then drawing as many as were needed. A main topic of discussion in each survey was home improvements. In the first round of interviews we found that slightly over a third (36 percent) of the households had made improvements on their houses. A year later this proportion had doubled: twenty-two families, or two-thirds of the sample, had improved their houses since December 1979. Of the eleven families who had not made improvements, seven said they planned to do so the following year.

The dramatic and unique nature of self-improvement generated by the 8 de Diciembre upgrading project is even more clear in comparison with similar areas of La Paz. My assistants visited three other neighborhoods that had not been upgraded. Like 8 de Diciembre, these communities were situated on the hillsides (laderas) of La Paz and had been settled for roughly twenty years. They were without water and sewerage systems and were served by footpaths rather than vehicle-bearing streets. In each area, a rapid visual survey with minimal interviewing was done of 200 randomly selected houses to see how many had been improved in the previous three years. In the three neighborhoods an average of 12 percent of the houses had been improved, whereas in 8 de Diciembre 67 percent of the households had made improvements (see table 3).

This large expenditure of energy and capital on home improvement was especially striking in the context of the rapidly deteriorating economic conditions in Bolivia during the period of project execution, particularly from February 1982 to December 1983. During the year in which this study was conducted, salaries in La Paz were estimated to have lost half their buying power. Despite this economic difficulty, the proportion of households in 8 de Diciembre making home improvements at least doubled, from one-third to two-thirds.[2]

The drama of this neighborhood's self-improvement in the throes of an economic crisis can be explained by both social and economic factors. Although they grumbled about project delays and the insensitivity of project staff, the great majority of the residents of this upgrading project were definitely satisfied with the improvements made in their neighborhood. Our intensive survey of 15 percent of the residents of the improved portion of 8 de Diciembre in April 1983 found that all thirty-three families interviewed said they planned to stay where they were living for the foreseeable future.

This loyalty to the area is striking in view of the great appreciation in land

Table 3. Home Improvements, 8 de Diciembre, December 1979 to April 1983

Improvement	Number	Percent
House completely rebuilt	9	27
Story added	3	9
One or two rooms added	4	12
Steps or facade improved	6	18
No improvements	11	33
Total	33	100

values—from 120 to 5,000 pesos ($5 to $24) per square meter—brought about by the project. For the average landholding in 8 de Diciembre of approximately 250 square meters, the value had thus increased $4,750 (850,000 pesos), the equivalent of average wages for more than seventy-seven months. Yet despite this very large increase in land value among a population for the most part impoverished,[3] not one family during the year of this study wanted to trade in their land and home for cash with which they could settle in a cheaper, presumably unserviced area and buy an income-generating good such as a bus, truck, or machinery. Although this phenomenon may be explained in part by a low demand for real estate during a time of economic recession, prospective buyers came to 8 de Diciembre each weekend. Rather, I sensed that with major improvements, people felt a strong and growing attachment to their barrio.

By providing water, sewerage, and street widening, the project enhanced the residents' pride in 8 de Diciembre and gave official recognition that both the neighborhood and the people who lived there were worthy of improvement. The natural response of the people was to affirm this recognition. One way to do this was to improve their living quarters; another was to stay in the neighborhood rather than sell the houses that had now become more valuable.

The degree to which people associate the conditions of their neighborhoods with their own identity may be seen in the story of a family I came to know well during my stays in 8 de Diciembre. The family was among the community's middle-class minority and lived in a neighborhood which at that time lacked street paving, street lights, and water and sewerage systems. Shortly after I arrived, the family gave a gala party to celebrate a daughter's fifteenth birthday, which according to Latin American custom is the occasion of a girl's initiation into womanhood. They had gone to the expense of printing invitations, which announced the party would be held in the house of an uncle in the more affluent barrio of Sopocachi, adjoining 8 de Diciembre. Some weeks after the party the father of the girl admitted that the family had chosen not to have the party in their own home in large part because of embarrassment over the poor conditions of 8 de Diciembre and the inconvenience guests would suffer from the muddy streets. This sense of the neighborhood's inferiority was more pronounced among the middle-class minority but permeated most of the area's residents; it began to disappear, however, as the area improved.

Urban services are, in this sense, rather like clothing; in addition to having a purely functional value, they convey status. It was common to hear people say, "before this project, 8 de Diciembre was an unserviced barrio;

now we are a part of the city proper." One community leader commented, "now we are respectable people [*somos gente*]."

Home improvements also generate employment. The self-help aspect of home improvement did not mean that homeowners did all the construction work themselves. Only one of the twenty-two families of the sample who had improved their houses did so only with its own labor. Most (thirteen) families used only paid labor; the remainder used a combination of paid workers and their own efforts. Since most of these people were self-employed as artisans, street vendors, taxi drivers, and the like, the opportunity cost of their time was too high to spend many hours working on their own houses. Typically, they hired underemployed construction workers, bricklayers, carpenters, and painters. Home improvement thus had beneficial effects on the informal sector of the city's economy, where it is often difficult to create opportunities for employment.

Another significant effect of upgrading was to increase the number of rental units in 8 de Diciembre. People who knew the area well estimated that in late 1979, at the time of project inception, roughly 30 percent of the households were occupied entirely or in part by renters. A door-to-door survey in July 1983 revealed that 179 out of 244 project households, or 80 percent, had renters. In March 1982 average monthly rent charged to tenants in 8 de Diciembre was between 1,500 and 2,000 pesos, or roughly one-third of the area's average family income of 4,916 pesos. Rent was thus an important source of income, especially in an economy in which income from other sources was diminishing. One resident said he had planned to sell his house, move to an inexpensive and unserviced part of town, and buy a truck to generate income. Instead, he borrowed money from relatives to add two rental units to his home and stayed in 8 de Diciembre. His story was eloquent testimony that rent is an important source of income and a stabilizer of the community.

Renters in 8 de Diciembre fell into two broad categories, those who lived in units owned by absentee landlords and those, like myself, who lived on the same premises as their landlords. The proportion of tenants with absentee landlords declined during the project because so many residents expanded their houses to make rental space. As I got to know tenants well enough to be invited into their homes it became apparent that those living with their landlords had better lighting and were more apt to have water and sewer connections[4] and more pleasant grounds than those who lived in quarters owned by absentee landlords. The reason was simple. When a tenant lives near his or her landlord it is far easier to express a desire for better service or register a complaint than when, as typically occurs with absentee landlords, the only communication is through a rent collector who visits once a month. It is also far less costly to extend a water or sewer line from one part of a house to another than from the main line in the street to the rental unit, as would be necessary in quarters occupied solely by renters. As one landlord expressed it: "I have had two renters in my house, one for four years, the other six years. I know them both well. I plan to build them a bathroom when the project puts in a water system. That's the right thing to do." The landlord who lives with tenants is more likely to improve tenant quarters because the improvement tends to enhance his own general living area as well.

The project indirectly helped promote live-in landlords and thus a better situation for renters. It stimulated an expansion of the city's rental housing stock, which is of particular importance to very poor families. Since most of the rental housing in the project was built by resident landlords, it was of a higher quality than most rental housing in La Paz, where absentee-landlord rental units prevail. By inducing more and better rental units, the project had both quantitative and qualitative catalytic effects here.

A story illustrates the catalytic effect of improved conditions for renters. Next door to where I lived was a large ramshackle house in dilapidated condition. My landlord had a running dispute with one of the neighbor's sons because of the young man's habit of lobbing rocks, for no apparent reason, onto my landlord's tin roof at around three o'clock in the morning, which woke everyone up. The boy, I soon learned, was mentally retarded. His father, mother, and brother were unemployed alcoholics. The father, who was also a paralytic, died during my second month in the barrio. The only source of income for the household was from twelve renters who paid small amounts totaling approximately 12,000 pesos ($60) in early 1983, about the average household monthly income for 8 de Diciembre at the time. At the end of my second stay in 8 de Diciembre, in April 1983, workmen began constructing a new wall of cement blocks between the tenement house and the street. One of the tenants explained to me that "This is the last house on this street not to have a wall. Finally the landlord decided that we too would improve our lot." If even the owner of this unfortunate abode was contracting labor to better her house, it seemed a significant sign that the self-improvement process initiated by this project had thoroughly permeated the area.

As mentioned earlier, the project worked far better at fostering individual or family self-help than it did at generating significant improvements for the community beyond the confines of the household plot. On my most recent visit to La Paz, in August 1984, I was disheartened to see most streets still unpaved, the community center still nonexistent, the channeling of the garbage-laden river still incomplete. Our mid-1983 survey showed that residents considered all of these improvements to be much needed. Various members of the community ascribed this lack of community self-help to poor leadership and insufficient motivation to do the required work. The elected president of the Neighborhood Committee, the most persistent and vociferous critic of the project, was not able to mobilize labor or delegate responsibility. He was an authoritarian, individualistic leader; either he did a job himself through his personal contacts, or it did not get done. The people, preoccupied with their own problems as the economic situation worsened, did not become a volunteer force of community workers as the project managers had expected.

A catalytic process of project development can be thought of as three-staged: first, the impetus provided by the project; second, the improvements carried out by beneficiaries but not financed by the project; third, neighborhood or community development. The third, clearly the most difficult, presupposes an identification of the individual's interest with the well-being of many. Social cohesion depends on this recognition of interdependent, collective self-interest.

One third-phase achievement in 8 de Diciembre in 1983 was the establishment of a consumer cooperative, which lowered the prices of staple foods for area residents. This communal initiative warranted explanation. Pablo, the individual with whom I had the closest rapport in the neighborhood, gave a reason that showed the potential for self-improvement at all three levels: "This project gave 8 de Diciembre its own identity. Without the streets and the water and sewerage systems we would have been absorbed into the community of Cristo Rey or another neighboring area. Out of this identity and the need created by the present economic crisis came the idea and later the establishment of the consumer cooperative to lower the prices of our basic foods."

Credit Programs

The urban projects in both La Paz and Guayaquil had major credit components. In La Paz the credit was primarily for artisans; it was provided by the upgrading executing unit, HAM-BIRF, and the Industrial Bank, BISA. In Guayaquil there was also an artisan credit program, administered by the Banco del Pacífico, and a small loan program for home improvements targeted at households in low-income communities of the city, executed by the Ecuadorian Housing Bank.

Credit is the least interventionist component of the urban projects reviewed here and, I believe, largely for that reason, the most successful component. Credit stimulates initiative that may be absent in more ambitious interventions, such as upgrading or new housing. Although credit is best when accompanied by good technical assistance, even alone credit generated profits and employment among artisans in La Paz and Guayaquil. The qualitative interviewing of the borrowers—low-income artisans in both La Paz and Guayaquil and home improvers in Guayaquil—did not reveal precise changes in income and in other economic indicators caused by the projects, as more traditional quantitative surveys utilizing control groups might have done. These in-depth interviews did, however, provide insight into how small entrepreneurs and low-income homeowners regarded the credit from the projects and used it to improve their own conditions. In this case, the borrowers—the beneficiaries of the project—became the primary catalysts of change.

Artisan Credit

Our evaluation of artisan credit programs was more tentative and rudimentary in La Paz than in Guayaquil. Sample sizes were small in both places.[5] Most artisan borrowers in La Paz and Guayaquil were tailors, woodworkers, shoemakers, and seamstresses. Artisans in each city were found to have increased their earnings and the number of employees. The average number of loans per artisan was 2.2 (a total of roughly $2,500). The lifetimes of loans received varied from six months to four years. According to very general estimates by the artisans themselves, earnings went up by two-fifths to three-fourths during the period and employment in the enterprises increased, on average, by two-fifths as a result of receiving credit from the projects. For these small enterprises, employing two to four workers, the program provided a major economic boost since the artisans would not otherwise have had access to scarce capital at even near market rates.

The survey showed clearly that the artisans who received credit in both cities were very much in favor of this program. Over 95 percent of the samples wanted to take out additional loans. This was to be expected, since the interest rates of these loans, at 12 percent annually, were far less than curb-side rates, which were as high as 1 percent a day, 360 percent annually. The artisan credit program reached persons generally excluded from the formal banking system, most not having received credit from any source before this project.

Of the 100 artisan borrowers interviewed in Guayaquil, less than a third had ever received credit before, less than a quarter from banks. The lack of readily accessible alternative sources of credit is reflected in the responses. A third of the sample said they had not had a prior loan either because they had not known where to borrow or because there had been no credit available. Of the seventy-one artisans in the sample who had not borrowed before, a fifth said the main reason was the onerous terms available elsewhere; a quarter of them stated that they had not wanted to get into debt because of the widespread fear of legal action against defaulters by banks. It is significant that this program managed to attract such recalcitrant borrowers.

Not only did the Banco del Pacífico manage to attract artisans to credit and to banking, but in many cases the credit launched their businesses on a successful new course even though they remained small. One of the artisans who had never before received a bank loan was a shoemaker in downtown Guayaquil. His eyes gleamed as he spoke of the promise of even brighter days ahead for his active workshop. When he had first taken out a loan from the Banco del Pacífico in 1978, he had just one employee; at the time of the interviews in September 1982 he had seven. Before the first of three loans from the program, his sales had been small. Currently he was providing footware to retail outlets in Guayaquil and in six other cities, some in neighboring provinces. Had his business improved with the credit? He replied, "Yes, 400 percent. I can honestly say that I would be producing nowhere near what I am today had I not obtained this credit. With it I've bought the machinery I needed to produce the quality and quantity of shoes the market demands." His next loan, he said, would allow him to buy another machine.

Although one of the most successful of the artisans interviewed, this man was like the majority in seeing himself as part of a growing, functioning business enterprise, whereas before the loan he had merely been an individual trying to make a meager living. The status conferred on him as a recipient of World Bank funds and the new responsibilities for paying them back had led to a more systematic method of keeping accounts, managing purchases, estimating market demand, promoting sales, and, as indicated by his statement, preparing to obtain more credit for investment in machinery and further expansion of production and earnings. As the bank in Ecuador, like BISA and HAM-BIRF in La Paz, reached out and drew the artisans into a formal system of both benefits and obligations, it encouraged individual initiative and helped to create self-sustaining entrepreneurs.[6] Just as a teacher may spark only two or three students to become creative, model leaders in their professions, so the kind of credit program described here may encourage only a small number of the largely neglected low-income majority. But this small number may well justify the efforts and the costs.

The cost of administering those small loans was not met by the 12 percent interest paid by the artisans. Although the World Bank had consistently urged higher interest rates so that the program would be self-supporting, 12 percent was as high as Ecuadorian credit regulations allowed. The artisan borrowers in both Guayaquil and La Paz were less than 3 percent in arrears, and almost all (95 percent) of those asked in Guayaquil said they would be willing to pay the 18 percent that Banco del Pacífico officials estimated would cover the costs of operation.[7]

Artisans may appear anachronistic in the modern, mechanized economies of the developed world, but they show every sign of maintaining their importance in the developing world. The artisan represents creative entrepreneurial energy, exemplified by the shoemaker in Guayaquil, which in developing countries has not yet been fully catalyzed and which warrants support. All but one of the Guayaquil artisans sampled increased profits during the time they were borrowers in the Banco del Pacífico loan program, twelve of them by more than 75 percent.

Home Improvement Loans

The home improvement loan program administered by the Ecuadorian Housing Bank (BEV) was the first in the history of Ecuador. It provided funds at prevailing bank rates to low-income persons who had never before had access to this kind of capital. The homeowners reacted very favorably to the credit; most wanted additional loans, and they used the funds in a number of economically progressive ways. In November 1982 my team interviewed a representative sample of 57 borrowers, 15 percent of the 380 households who had received checks from January to July 1982. The borrowers were located in the poorest areas of Guayaquil, primarily Suburbio and Guasmo; most (81 percent) did not have title to their land. Loan sizes averaged 36,570 sucres ($914) and were limited to 30,000 sucres ($1,000) for unmortgaged properties and roughly twice this amount for mortgaged properties.

Forty-four percent used their loans to build a new house; almost the same proportion used them to add one or two rooms or a second story.[8] With construction of this magnitude, it is understandable that only one family out of fifty-six respondents found the loan large enough to cover the entire cost of improvement. The average loan covered little more than a quarter of the average total outlay for house construction of 128,218 sucres ($3,205). The program helped stimulate or, to some degree, leverage capital at a ratio of approximately 4:1. It was not clear to what degree the loan served as an incentive for additional and greater expenditure and to what degree it merely complemented something already planned or started. Personal observation and conversation with about half of those interviewed leads me to conclude that both purposes were served and the two are not easily separable. Certainly, the receipt of a loan gave some people more of an incentive to make home improvements or even replace a structure than they would have had in the absence of the program.

Because these loans represented only a small proportion of total outlays for home construction, it was difficult to determine the degree to which the loan generated employment. Borrowers stated that they used two-thirds of the loan amount, or an average of 24,814 sucres ($260), to pay the costs of labor. (This amount is the equivalent of six minimum monthly wages.) The vast majority—fifty-one of fifty-seven borrowers in the sample—used paid labor in their home construction. Only six of the fifty-seven borrowers qualified as self-helpers in the full sense of using only unremunerated family labor. Twice this number (21 percent) supervised the construction themselves. Often the borrowers employed friends or family to help with the construction and keep labor costs down; about half the hired hands fit in this category, while the rest were outsiders.

Clearly the loan program met a financial need of homeowners in low-income settlements. There did not appear to have been any credit available in Guayaquil for home improvement on terms comparable to those offered by this program of BEV and the World Bank. The additional capital the borrowers needed came generally from their personal savings (used by 96 percent of the borrowers). As further testimony of the utility of this program, 79 percent of the sample planned to take out another loan from BEV in the future. In addition, the Guayaquil home improvement program, like the La Paz upgrading program, encouraged the addition of rental units, thereby increasing the housing stock and generating needed income for the homeowner. Over a quarter of the sample intended to rent part or all of the additional space they were building with loan funds. The average monthly income of the sixteen families that expressed a desire to rent was 8,444 sucres ($211), roughly two-thirds of the income of those who had no intention of renting.

The two chief problems with the program came from inadequate outreach into the city's low-income communities. First, the beneficiaries were not among the city's poorest residents despite their location in poor neighborhoods. Average monthly family income (11,264 sucres, or $287) was about 45 percent more than the median for the city and 25 percent more than the upper-income limit for program eligibility. Second, more than a quarter (28 percent) of the sample were behind in their monthly payments. Understandably, the first persons to take advantage of the new Housing Bank loan program were the least poor persons in the low-income areas of the city, many of whom had apparently underreported their income to gain access to loan capital. Credit and banking generally are still alien to the poor in a city like Guayaquil. And it is not uncommon in government loan programs targeted at the poor for many people to fall behind in their payments, especially during the early phases of a program. The problem in Guayaquil, however, was again one of communication: the lower-income people had not been given enough information—many did not know about the program, and some of those who did take out loans did not understand their repayment obligations. Largely as a result of these findings, BEV-BIRF, the implementation unit, has decided to extend its outreach into the low-income areas of Guayaquil where its borrowers live. By establishing a network of branch offices it hopes to promote the program and improve collection services.

Much of the data on the home improvement program has been quantitative. Qualitative interviews, however, were particularly well suited to explore the catalytic effect of the credit program on the purchase of building materials, the utilization of labor, and the creation of rental units. People who had improved their homes with loans from this program expressed singular pride in their achievement. Even more than one's neighborhood one's house is an extension of oneself. Home improvement is thus seen by the people as a form of self-improvement. On numerous occasions homeowners walked me through the improved areas of their houses explaining how it had looked before and revealing plans for future loans.

For persons with unstable employment in low-status occupations who see themselves living in an often alien world, the home takes on particular importance as a source of relief, security, and sense of self-respect. The house is also a family's major asset. Improvements can create space for rent or for commercial use (such as a workshop or retail outlet) or can simply add to the owner's capital base. The home improvements brought about by this loan program in Guayaquil occurred because the project built on deep-seated human and economic values for home and its physical manifestation, housing.

Core Housing

The *piso-techo* (floor-roof) component of the Guayaquil project appeared to incorporate much of what this chapter has been about: individual initiative, incremental growth, and the value of housing. Executed by the Ecuadorian Housing Bank, this pilot program was designed to provide inexpensive semi-completed housing that low-income people could afford and could finish building according to their own preferences and financial capabilities. As the name implies, the piso-techo unit consisted of a floor, a roof, two side walls, and a toilet. The unit covered roughly a third of a lot of 90 square meters. The residents were expected to use their own resources to add front and back walls, doors and windows, and inner partitions. There were 104 such units built in Floresta adjacent to the completed houses of the Guaya-quil project.

The concept was simple but, it is now apparent, inappropriate. It was thought that people who could not easily afford the completed structures provided by the project (15,000 sucres for the down payment and 2,100 sucres a month) could pay the reduced cost of the piso-techo unit (10,000 sucres for the down payment and 1,700 sucres a month). Over time, the piso-techo dwellers were expected to improve their houses while living in them, using makeshift methods and inexpensive materials such as bamboo.

At the time of my second stay in Guayaquil, in July 1983, five months after the project executing unit had handed over the piso-techo units for occupancy, half of the houses (fifty-one, or 49 percent) were unoccupied; twenty of these had had no improvements whatsoever. We interviewed a sample of twenty-four piso-techo households (23 percent of the total) in their new homes in Floresta or, in the case of those who had not yet moved, in their current homes. The previous year, before the units were built, interviews had been conducted with persons selected for this project. The message of both sets of interviews was the same: most of the piso-techo beneficiaries preferred to finish building their houses with good materials and often took advantage of the opportunity to enlarge the core unit; but many could not afford to complete the structures that they wanted. Rather than move into a partially completed, makeshift dwelling, they preferred to stay where they were until they had accumulated enough capital to make the desired additions.

Many of the families selected for the piso-techo housing were too poor to afford the additions they felt were necessary. If it is assumed that the income of these families increased at the same rate as that recorded for the other Floresta samples from November 1982 to July 1983, the piso-techo families would have been earning an average of 9,192 sucres ($97) a month. For twenty-one piso-techo families interviewed who had either built or made estimates of what it would cost to build their units as they wanted, the average cost of additions to the semi-finished core was 105,619 sucres ($1,112), or 11.5 times their average monthly salary. Thus it took about a year's wages to complete the piso-techo units, according to actual experiences and plans of this pilot project.

In a time of decreasing purchasing power, money available for housing in Guayaquil was in ever diminishing supply. From mid-1982 to mid-1983, the period of this evaluation, inflation in Ecuador was approximately 60 percent. The prices of many basic foodstuffs rose at far higher rates than this (see table 4). Conversations with several informants revealed dramatic increases that averaged well over 100 percent at a time when people's salaries rose less than 20 percent on the average. No wonder many families earning less than $100 a month could not scrape together the $1,000 needed to complete their houses to what they deemed to be the minimal standard. Indeed, it is testimony to the importance of housing that half of these poor families in such dire economic times were able to find the resources necessary to complete their structures.

The problem with the piso-techo program was not its reliance on incremental construction, which is a normal practice in urban settlements of low-income persons in Latin America.[9] Rather, the program appeared to underestimate the amount of money needed both to maintain the beneficiaries' existing rental quarters and to pay for labor and materials to make the unit habitable. The largest single source of capital for piso-techo completion was personal savings. Eight of the twenty-one families making or planning improvements cited this as their only source. Another three had access to family funds for their construction. Only three of the twenty-one families had access to bank loans. Another six received loans from their places of work. For roughly half of the piso-techo families their own savings were simply not enough, and there was nowhere else to go to supplement the little they had. The frustration of having a partially completed structure waiting to be occupied was voiced by a woman in her hot two-room apartment in a downtown slum: "We want very much to move to our

Table 4. Food Prices in Guayaquil, 1982–83

| | | Price (sucres) | |
Food	Quantity	June 1982	June 1983
Sugar	1 pound	7	20
Rice	1 pound	5	15
Tomatoes	1 pound	7	15
Meat	1 pound	30	60
Eggs	1 pound	2	6
Milk	1 liter	10	20

house, to leave this crowded place, but we have to keep paying rent here and we just don't have the money to complete the house so that we can live in it."

A significant corollary finding has come from one of the second generation of World Bank–initiated qualitative evaluations (discussed in chapter 6) halfway around the world in Thailand, where World Bank–funded projects provided incomplete serviced core units similar to Guayaquil's piso-techo units. Local researchers have discovered the same phenomenon of land and semi-completed structures lying idle and unoccupied for as much as eighteen months because the owners had no access to credit to finish the house as they desired. In the Nong Hoy site in the northern city of Chiang Mai in April 1985, sixteen months after the lots and semi-completed houses had been purchased, only about 50 percent of the 827 units were occupied and about another 140 (17 percent) were still being worked on by the owners and laborers hired by them. Thus, after well over a year, one-third of the units that had been bought remained half-finished shells. In the larger Tung Song Hong site in Bangkok the story was better but still problematic; after twelve months of possession about 75 percent of the 612 families of the first phase had moved into their units. Again, a quarter of the households had not been able to meet the financial burden of buying the building materials and paying for the labor to complete their houses as they wished. In a survey of fifty families in Nong Hoy done by the University of Chiang Mai "not one family was happy about the expandable core concept." In the words of one low-income resident of the project, "these houses are not designed for poor people like us."[10]

In both Ecuador and Thailand, as a result of the information provided by this participant-observer evaluation, credit is now being provided to the owners of incomplete core units to help them finish their houses and move in more quickly. It is worthwhile to explore the error in judgment that was made in these projects. Planners assumed that people might move in within one or two months, perhaps first completing the piso-techo units with bamboo walls and then gradually finishing the house with more permanent materials. In Guayaquil, it does not seem that the people's own ideas had been given sufficient consideration in the design of the project. In a randomly selected sample of 54 of the 510 families who were to occupy the World Bank–supported Floresta project approximately three-quarters of those interviewed expressed a preference for completed over incomplete structures. Among families allotted the piso-techo units only somewhat over half (56 percent) were pleased with this solution, compared with an 86 percent satisfaction rate among those who were to live in the completed units. The advantages of the completed house are immediate occupancy and freedom from the need for additional construction. These advantages appeared to outweigh the piso-techo unit's advantages of flexibility in the style and construction of the finished house and lower monthly mortgage payments.

The Ecuadorian Housing Bank designed the piso-techo house to reach poorer families, in response to the criticism that its previous houses were affordable only to families earning approximately 9,000 sucres ($155) monthly—considered a middle-class income in Ecuador. The low-income beneficiaries for whom the piso-techo housing was intended, however, believed that these houses were more suitable for more affluent persons who had the capital needed to complete the units. The felt need for better quality of construction was particularly acute in Floresta, where the unfinished structures were flanked on one side by the mostly bamboo houses of Guasmo, which the piso-techo owners wanted their houses to surpass, and on the other sides by the 2,500 completed houses of the project, whose standards they wanted at least to match.

Lessons

Catalytic effects occur when a project builds on people's demonstrated values. Where people live and work is an indication of what they value. In providing loans for upgrading communities and credit for artisans and homeowners, the projects encouraged people to follow their natural wishes and stimulated processes already in motion. Moreover, beneficiaries most appreciated the project components that channeled the energy and initiative which were already apparent. These components were, after all, a positive recognition and reinforcement of what the people had demonstrated was important to them.

The piso-techo program, however, imposed a solution that the designers thought would be best, particularly with regard to housing type and income constraints. And the people did not act as the designers assumed they would. Although there were families in Guayaquil (and in Thailand) who lived up to expectations by moving onto the site within the first few months and completing their houses with less costly materials, at least as many needed more time and money than expected because they had less access to credit and wanted to build at higher standards than expected. Factors such as peer pressure and pride in quality work were not taken into account by project designers. One conclusion from this analysis—albeit tentative because of the small base of the three project sites—is that projects should provide small and habitable units with access to credit to allow for immediate occupancy and expansion over time.

The policy conclusion that may be drawn from this analysis of catalytic effects is that a project's success is directly related to how much encouragement is given to people's ongoing self-improvement processes. Project activities in which people have little self-help experience, such as the community work in 8 de Diciembre or the completion of new, unfinished housing in Floresta, cannot succeed without extensive promotion and often material incentives, such as credit. Projects that are successful draw on people's expressed desire for self-advancement in ways that expand opportunities for it to take place. In La Paz and Guayaquil the infrastructure to upgrade the community and the provision of credit led to home improvements, which in turn provided jobs and more rental housing of better quality for low-income persons. Artisans' credit led to increased employment. In projects that supply new housing, as in upgrading projects, if catalytic development is to occur, public authorities should facilitate the owners' efforts to build additions to their houses for rental purposes.

« 5 »

THE PROJECT CONTEXT:
WHEN, WHERE, WHO

A development project, to be successful, must come at the right time in the right place and be right for the people for whom it is intended. Too often the view from above, where a project planner or manager sits, fails to comprehend the historical, geographical, and social context of a project that may stand in the way of project objectives. In both Guayaquil and La Paz, the view from the ground revealed horizons not visible from above.

Historical Context

In the La Paz project, 8 de Diciembre had not been among the first neighborhoods chosen for improvement. Five other very poor neighborhoods on the laderas of La Paz had originally been selected for upgrading. In a story similar to that of Guasmo Norte in Guayaquil, the La Paz neighborhoods had at first accepted, then refused to allow the project. In this case the overt issue was the principle of cost recovery, but the underlying political opposition was just as important.

The municipality had previously done minor upgrading works in the five neighborhoods, some involving community labor. None of the projects, however, entailed such extensive change as was planned for the World Bank project. Moreover, for the first time, the municipality required the residents to pay for the upgrading over time. At the time of project appraisal by the World Bank in 1976, the community organizations in all five barrios agreed to the controversial principle of cost recovery. After several years of delay in getting the project under way, however, the neighborhoods rescinded their agreement to pay. The project was aborted just as the municipality was finally ready to contract for construction of civil works.

In my discussions with the project director, I learned that the leaders of the first five areas selected opposed the municipal government of the time. In talking to their constituencies, these local leaders criticized the cost-recovery aspect of the project as an example of government exploitation of the poor and demanded that the improvements should be free. With the benefit of hindsight, this issue, like many others, seems obvious. Had the project planners grasped the history of antagonism between the municipality and each community, they might have avoided the controversy by promoting the project more extensively within the barrios and, more important, in the city at large so that neighborhoods willing to pay could benefit from the project.

In 8 de Diciembre, which was subsequently offered the upgrading project and carried it through with great success, the local leadership was not only willing to cooperate with the municipality, but it had been seeking this kind of improvement project for as long as nine years. I came upon these key historical facts after I had been living in 8 de Diciembre almost two months. It was April and the rainy season was over. The streets that had been muddy for months were now dusty under the intense sun of the Bolivian Altiplano. One evening my friend Pablo sent his son to my room to ask me to join him. Pablo was at the door when I arrived: "There is someone I know you'd like to meet. He lives just down the road. I have told him of your work, and he would like to talk with you."

The man and his wife welcomed us. We began to discuss the upgrading project. The house, the couple's dress, the wine they offered, and their opinions of the project clearly established them as one of the few middle-class households of the neighborhood. This family had lived in 8 de Diciembre almost fifteen years. The man had once been actively involved in attempts to improve the community: "I was president of the Neighborhood Committee in 1971–72, and we tried back then to get the municipality to provide us with physical infrastructure, but not enough of the families cared. Most were peasants or renters. The former were used to the country-side, the latter felt improvements would raise their rents. At that time most of the land was owned by six absentee landlords." Pablo corroborated his neighbor's account of these upgrading overtures a decade before the project began. Later I was given access to the Neighborhood Committee's archives and discovered correspondence with the mayor's office in which the Neighborhood Committee had again requested water and sewer systems in September 1977, three years before negotiations for the project began.

The local leadership is one key factor, as discussed in chapter 3. Just as important is the point in the history of a place when a project intervenes. In Guasmo Norte and in the first neighborhoods selected in La Paz, the project was bucking an adverse tide; in 8 de Diciembre tide and current were with the project. For development to succeed it should enhance ongoing progressive trends. To discover where such trends do and do not exist, one needs to be aware of local history.

Location

Life in an urban development site is conditioned by the bordering areas, particularly those which are unimproved. When one area receives benefits such as water and sewerage and contiguous areas do not, the imbalance creates friction between the residents, political pressure for remedies by the unimproved areas, and a strain on the resources available.

One afternoon in 8 de Diciembre I walked across the Duraznani River into the neighboring settlement of Jinchupalla, which had not participated in the improvement project. I caught up to two children in their early teens who lived in Jinchupalla and had just visited a cousin in 8 de Diciembre. One expressed puzzlement and discontent with the improvements in 8 de Diciembre. "My cousin has running water and a bathroom in her house and yet we who live so close have neither in our house," she said. "Why is this? It doesn't seem fair."

Months later, during one of my first days in the public housing project of Floresta in Guayaquil, I again listened to a young resident. This time the tone was impassioned: "Last week a gang of young men came over from Guasmo [the large unserviced slum next to Floresta] and stole things from several houses on our walkway. Residents of Floresta quickly got together and defended themselves and the gang left, but one of them was killed and others on both sides were wounded."

8 de Diciembre

When the upgrading project began in La Paz in late 1981, well over half (70 percent) of the families in the formally designated area of 8 de Diciembre were living outside the subdistrict selected for the project. These 500 families lived either in Jinchupalla to the south of the project area or in 8 de Diciembre Alto to the west and up the hill (see map 2).

The exclusion of these groups was done not by design but rather out of an understandable, if unfortunate, process of selection. The topographical features of Jinchupalla and the Zona Alta would have made improvement work more costly than in the selected area. Jinchupalla was on less solid land and the Zona Alta was more steeply inclined than the part of 8 de Diciembre to be upgraded. In addition the residents of the two settlements were poorer, which would have made the collection of payments for project expenses more difficult. The area of 8 de Diciembre that received the upgrading presented fewer physical problems and was also the place of residence of all the community leaders.

Only after the project agreement was signed with the 220 community residents did Jinchupalla become organized and begin pressing for inclusion in the project. The smaller area of the Zona Alta did not actively petition for inclusion until prompted to do so, at least in part as a result of being included in the socioeconomic questionnaire for the present evaluation. From my discussions with all parties, it appears that neither HAM-BIRF, the executing agency, nor the existing Neighborhood Committee made a concerted effort at the time of project negotiations, in mid-1979, to incorporate Jinchupalla and the Zona Alta into the project.

A third excluded area was along the Cotahuma River, which divides 8 de Diciembre from the affluent neighborhood of Sopocachi to the north and east and thus separates the hitherto unserviced low-income neighborhood from the respectable part of the city. It was and is the worst single physical feature of the neighborhood. In times of heavy rain, it has eaten away the soil at its edges, making the needed (and promised) improvements to streets and the provision of water and sewerage for houses along the river's edge difficult if not impossible. In addition, this river has traditionally served as a latrine and garbage dump for residents, not only of 8 de Diciembre but elsewhere too. It is a breeding place for flies and vermin. The river's smell alone should have convinced anyone interested in the betterment of the area that it needed attention. The project as such did not include improvements for the river, although the Neighborhood Committee attempted to persuade the municipality's civil works division to undertake channeling of the river in conjunction with the project. This petition initially met with a favorable response. For roughly a third of the river's course along the borders of 8 de Diciembre, it had been channeled through a paved, sluiced river bed with walls to contain erosion. At the time of my second stay in the area, in April 1983, this salutary labor had unfortunately been halted for close to a year.

The practical reasons for excluding the two contiguous settlements and the Cotahuma River from the upgrading project could have been weighed against other important factors, but their significance to the residents was revealed only by a better understanding of the area. The excluded areas were certainly more difficult to upgrade, physically and socially, than the project area. Channeling the river was an expensive undertaking, and money spent on it would be diverted from basic infrastructural work in other unserviced areas of the city. Nevertheless, after living in the area, I came to appreciate that improvements to the river and the neighboring settlements were important issues which the people of 8 de Diciembre saw as related to the upgrading project. It seemed that every week individuals or groups in these neighboring areas drew my attention to their plight and suggested various kinds of improvements for which they were willing to pay. Citywide as well as local political leaders were drawn into the effort to turn the improvement process into a more balanced and equitable effort. The representatives of the subcommittee of Jinchupalla told me that the mayor of La Paz had promised them during the local festival of December 8, 1981, that they would be included in the project. During my second stay in the area, a man was elected president of the Neighborhood Committee largely on the strength of his promise that both contiguous areas would soon be improved.

Floresta

The decision to locate the new housing area of Floresta next to the sprawling squalor of Guasmo may well have been more serious than the inattention to the bordering areas of 8 de Diciembre. Some perspective on this awkward juxtaposition of Floresta and Guasmo may be gained from a brief history of the area. In the late 1970s, as the military government in Ecuador was being replaced by a populist democratic regime, the southern region of Guayaquil, where Guasmo is located, became a major staging area for diverse political parties. Although the area is below sea level and largely mangrove swamps, it was the only remaining large piece of open land accessible to low-income families in Guayaquil. As such it was the site of massive invasions of poor families, the first of which was Guasmo Norte, site of the unsuccessful upgrading effort reported in chapter 3. This growing squatter population clamored for land tenure and demanded services from local and national politicians, each of whom promised more than the other, with far more rhetoric than concrete action. In response to the situation in Guasmo, the new president of Ecuador, Jaime Roldos, ordered the Ecuadorian Housing Bank to establish quickly a low-cost public housing program in Guayaquil. The first site chosen was Floresta, which was already owned by the Housing Bank but was being occupied by squatters. As late as the time of my stay in Guayaquil, from mid-1982 to early 1983, more squatters took over Housing Bank land adjacent to Floresta, erecting a placard at their site which read "Floresta III" (see map 4).

While I lived in Floresta I saw signs of growing conflict with its poorer, much larger neighbor. The general malaise and apprehensiveness of Floresta residents were due to the marked inequality between the services they received and those in Guasmo. In addition, there was pressure on the urban services (water supply, roads, and garbage collection) used by Floresta and by Guasmo residents. Water for Guasmo was drawn from main lines that served both areas and was transported by truck along roads used by both; this system lowered the water pressure in Floresta and contributed to the deterioration of road surfaces. Guasmo residents deposited their garbage in overladen receptacles in Floresta to take advantage of the collection service, which, though inadequate, was better than in Guasmo, where it was entirely absent.

The problems associated with this awkward coupling of a runaway slum and a fledgling would-be middle-class housing development depended very much on one's perspective. For Floresta residents it was annoying to enter the shower stall and find there was insufficient water pressure for a shower. Some neighbors blamed the situation on the trucks which took water from the city supply and sold it to the 200,000 persons in Guasmo. Others said the water shortage was endemic to the entire southern zone of the city in which we were located. From my talks with residents in other, more expensive housing areas of this zone, it appeared the problem was indeed general, though less acute elsewhere.

Security was also a serious issue for Floresta residents, who were often the victims of robbery, vandalism, and personal injury. The fear of crime was pervasive among my neighbors, many of whom had come from older, more homogeneous parts of the city. Although no section of Guayaquil is known for safety or tranquility, the proximity to the poorer neighbors of Guasmo was unsettling to many Floresta residents. At the first meeting of the walkway where I lived, in November 1982, two of the five suggested improvements were related to security: the recommendations that each house have a night-light facing the pathway and that a night watchman be hired to guard the area.[1]

The people of Guasmo had their own perspective on the fully serviced housing project being built at their very doorstep. From numerous conversations with Guasmo residents, it became clear that the presence of Floresta increased their desire for similar services. It is doubtful that infrastructure will reach this area in the near future, however, because of the political problems mentioned in chapter 3, together with the high cost of landfill—a precondition for major structural improvements—and the dire poverty of most of the households of Guasmo.

« »

In both La Paz and Guayaquil, improvements in the project areas created imbalances in the extent to which urban services were provided to contiguous neighborhoods. Much of the imbalance was unavoidable, in part for administrative reasons. In Guayaquil parallel authorities were responsible for the neighboring areas—the Housing Bank, a national agency, for Floresta and the municipality for Guasmo—and coordination between them was intrinsically poor. Financial constraints were even more crucial: there simply were not enough resources to go around to all who needed them. Still, administrative or financial constraints, however severe, should not prevent planners and managers from considering spatial location in relation to neighboring areas. Both those living on the project site and their neighbors on unimproved land are keenly aware that who gets what will have far-reaching effects on their everyday lives. And an area that, to a planner, may be off the drawing board is, to a beneficiary, a neighboring community.

Had planners and managers attended to the larger spatial context, they could have incorporated into the design of the projects a number of measures to alleviate the imbalance between project areas and bordering communities. In Guayaquil, the infrastructure project for Guasmo Norte, if it had not failed, would have been a positive step toward equalizing services between Floresta and its poorer neighbor. In addition, a health center or other community facility could have been constructed to serve the population of both Floresta and part of Guasmo. In La Paz, studies of land conditions and the feasibility of extending the project to contiguous areas could have been part of the improvement project. Funds for channeling the river could have been incorporated into the project as a government contribution. Despite inattention to the geographical context of these projects, administrators of both executing agencies, the municipality of La Paz and the Housing Bank in Guayaquil, were aware of the need for more comprehensive planning in the future. They agreed that representatives of surrounding areas should be included in discussions about the project, wherever feasible, and that eventually the project benefits should, if possible, be extended to those areas.

Social Context

If time and space may be considered the length and width of a project's fabric, the social dimension may be thought of as its texture. The farther one is from a beneficiary population, the less one appreciates the variety of the people affected, just as a plaid tweed might appear from a distance to be bland and of one color. The potential for development is directly related to an understanding of who is being developed, and planners may miss opportunities if they fail to understand important differences among the people a project is affecting. Three kinds of internal divisions among beneficiary groups in La Paz and Guayaquil seemed inadequately understood by project managers: proprietary, societal, and cultural.

Beneficiaries and Renters

It was natural that my first contacts in 8 de Diciembre would be with the local leadership, most of whom were middle class. These families had been instrumental in first seeking the project from the municipality, then serving as brokers between the public authorities and the community, and finally promoting the project among their neighbors. These articulate and civic-minded leaders were proud of the project, which they saw as a fruit of their own labor. They had even recorded on film the first heady experience of upgrading, when the entire neighborhood—fathers, mothers, and children—pitched in to help dig and fill ditches for the water and sewer pipes. They were anxious to talk with this foreigner who had come in their midst to learn about how they felt about the project.

I had been living in 8 de Diciembre about a month when I asked my friend Pablo about the people who lived in the small, modest row housing across the street from his more comfortable home. "Oh, those are renters," he said. "The landlord is the mother-in-law of Eduardo" (one of the most prominent of the local leaders). Upon further inquiry, I discovered that there were renters all through the neighborhood. Many lived in quarters owned by absentee landlords—persons who had never lived in 8 de Diciembre but owned land and rented houses for speculative purposes. Others, like myself, lived in a room on the same premises as the landlord.

The renters were virtually second-class citizens in the area. Not being homeowners they had not signed contracts with the project. But they constituted a large proportion of the area's overall population—roughly a third when I first arrived, and more than half when I left in mid-1983—and any claim to have improved living conditions in the area could not ignore them. Yet, because project staff had been unaware of the numerical signifi-cance of the renters, either actual or potential, and had little understanding of their living conditions, renters had been neglected in project planning.

Renting is not a phenomenon that is immediately apparent. Landlords sometimes do not mention their tenants to avoid taxation or other incur-sions by public authorities. Renters may not declare themselves as such to avoid the stigma of their inferior status or in deference to their landlord's silence on this matter.

Renters deserve attention in upgrading projects because their situation is greatly changed by a project of this sort. As shown by the experience in La Paz, the trend in upgrading is to increase both the quality and quantity of rental units (see chapter 4). The man who had been president of the 8 de Diciembre Neighborhood Committee in 1971–72 provided some data on the number of renters and owners in the area at that time. On the assump-tion that he was talking about the entire area of 8 de Diciembre, including Jinchupalla and the Zona Alta as well as the part that later was upgraded, and on the basis of my own estimates from survey data and interviews, the numbers of owners and renters changed over the decade as follows:

	Owners	Renters
1971	39	138
1983	320	810

After the upgrading, there were approximately two and a half times more new renters than new owners in 8 de Diciembre. Most renters, 570 of the 810, lived in the upgraded area, and more than half of these had moved in during the time of the upgrading project.

Given the facts that the new rental units represent additions to the city's housing stock, provide increased income to the homeowners who rent, and (being largely owner-occupied) have more amenities than the tenant quar-ters owned by absentee landlords (see chapter 4), an urban development program might well wish to provide credit to accentuate this trend to more and better rental accommodations. Although some credit for home improvement should be made available for all qualified homeowners in the area being upgraded, additional amounts could be given to borrowers who intend to construct one or more rental units.

Once I discovered the presence of this less visible subgroup, I made extra efforts to converse with renters and see how they viewed the changes in the community caused by the project. I found them to be indifferent or appre-hensive. Two renters whom I visited periodically were Juan, a tailor, and Raimundo, a mechanic. Both were underemployed because the demand for their services had decreased with the economic crisis in Bolivia. Juan lived with his wife and three children in one room. Raimundo, a younger man, had only his wife and a nephew in his one room. Four other families rented single rooms in their compound; all six families shared a central courtyard and one latrine. The owner lived in downtown La Paz. The two men felt the project had not helped them at all. "This project is for the homeowners," Juan told me, and "the Neighborhood Committee is for them too." But these men were not transients—Juan had lived in 8 de Diciembre nine years, Raimundo seven years.[2] In April 1982, when most of the beneficiaries' houses were still not connected to the water or sewer systems, I asked Juan and Raimundo whether they believed that their house or room would be connected. They did not think so, especially since the house was being sold in a few months.

During my second stay in 8 de Diciembre I found that a majority (58 percent) of a representative sample of 200 renter families living in the upgraded portion had not yet received the benefits of piped-in water and sewerage in their living quarters even though connections had been made in almost all of the homeowners' residences. Despite this lack of attention to the renters' basic needs, many of the landlords had been able to raise rents considerably in the previous twelve months because the general desirability of the area had increased. In some respects, however, renters were worse off than before. The public water taps had been removed from the upgraded area so they now had to walk across the river to the taps of Jinchupalla or, awkwardly, to beg water from neighbors. Now their second-class status was all the more pronounced, for it was only the renters who had to carry buckets of water up the often steeply inclined streets of 8 de Diciembre. Lacking toilets, the renters still used the river for their daily needs, thus negating much of the effort to improve sanitation in the area.

The project executing unit in La Paz, upon receiving information from this participant-observer evaluation, decided that all future signatories to contracts for upgrading improvements would be required to make the infrastructure accessible to any renters on the improved property. Although landlords will probably raise their rents to cover the costs of providing household connections, the additional increases would likely be minimal and would be more than offset by better sanitation for the entire area.

Renters are clearly a part of the social fabric that project managers and policymakers would be wise not to ignore. Yet, even though I was living in the area, it took me close to a month to become aware of the importance of renters in 8 de Diciembre. It takes time to become familiar with an area's population and to identify its main elements, but this knowledge is essential to have during both the planning and execution stages so that the project can incorporate the important subgroups in ways that promote both equity and development.

Women and Youth

Much of my activity while living in the project areas could be described as intensive market research for development. When the objective is to improve living conditions for a particular group on a cost-recovery basis, all members of the group are potential "customers" of the project. In both La Paz and Guayaquil, my primary associations were with the male heads of families. Through door-to-door interviews, conversations with young people on the street, and talks with my female assistants in both countries, however, I gradually became aware that both women and youths were sources of energy for development that were largely untapped by these projects.

Like many observations made here, this one is not presented as definitive or necessarily novel. Observations that come from such guided, informal inquiries are often most useful as hypotheses or perceptions which later more rigorous research and analysis may explore more fully. The reality in 8 de Diciembre was that women, who had the most immediate interest in the infrastructural improvements, and youths, who had the most time and energy, were conspicuously absent from the councils or meetings where decisions about the future of the area were made.

It was mainly women and children who carried pails of water from the public standpipes to the houses. The women were the ones who used the water for cooking and made sure their children used water for washing. The women had to clean up after the children in the absence of sewerage. Although few (10 percent) of the heads of households in 8 de Diciembre were women, close to half (41 percent) of the wives were wage earners. Almost all adult females had primary responsibility for household duties, raising the children, and often administering the budget as well.

The negotiations for how much rent I was to pay for my room in the barrio were not untypical. Although I dealt directly with the male head of household, his wife was at his side and before every step of the process he not only turned to her but clearly deferred to her judgment as to the amount of rent they found acceptable.

Both women and youths were conscious of being largely excluded from active participation in the Neighborhood Committee and wanted more involvement. In La Paz this was true in 8 de Diciembre and in two other project areas, 16 de Julio and San Antonio, where my two assistants lived for three months. The following remarks were not unusual. A woman in San Antonio commented on the heated discussions at committee meetings about acceptance of the project. "All the men do is argue, often for no reason but to hear themselves talk," she said. "If we women could make the decisions, we would have had water [that is, the project] long ago." Another woman in 8 de Diciembre spoke in the same vein: "When men get together to work they lay one stone and then start drinking." In sum, women spend more time in the neighborhood, are more aware of the relationship between sanitation and their children's health, are more burdened by the lack of good services, and are often more responsible (certainly more sober) than many of the men.

Young persons between the ages of fifteen and twenty-five appeared to participate in sports clubs, but in no other community activities. Yet youths were generally better educated than their parents. In San Antonio and 16 de Julio, most of the older persons had come from the country and many spoke Aymara or Quechua as a first language, whereas the youths spoke Spanish fluently and could have participated effectively in committee meetings or in dealings with the project implementation staff, since communication was always in Spanish. The young men in particular felt they were not wanted at the meetings presided over by the older men, yet they had constructive suggestions and ideas for improvement. A group of young people in San Antonio was seeking resources for a library, for example.

Mothers' clubs and sports clubs are the traditional associations of women and youths, respectively, in the barrios of La Paz. From our observation neither of these entities in the three low-income areas in which we lived was integrated into the community association. Largely as a result, they were not actively involved in the betterment of the areas. In 8 de Diciembre there was instead antagonism between officials of the sports league and the Neighborhood Committee. The league charged rent for the use of the community sports field by teams from other communities, but was reluctant to apply any of its considerable revenues to community needs that were not directly related to sports.

Inasmuch as all members of a community benefit from improvements such as infrastructure, it should be possible to enlist their support for a development project. By working through existing organizations and, if necessary, by creating new ones, the community leaders can involve the main subgroups of the population. Women may be enlisted to manage a consumer cooperative or help staff a day-care center or health facility. Youths could be reached through their sports clubs or other associations and encouraged to provide labor on community works, such as street paving or the building of a community center. The male heads of family who dominate the Neighborhood Committee would not be bypassed by female and youth involvement. On the contrary, the committee would be the central body that would delegate responsibility and coordinate the myriad activities in which all would participate. There is no recipe for this kind of comprehensive mobilization of a community. What will work in one place may not in another. In Latin America, women and youths do not tend to be borrowers or community leaders. Yet their energies certainly represent vital potential forces that could be harnessed for future community development.

The Cultures of Poverty

Most people in La Paz and Guayaquil are, in a real sense, poor. The median family income in La Paz and Guayaquil in 1982, when I began residing in each place, was roughly $150 and $190 a month, respectively. These figures declined at least 10 percent the following year. There are, however, various degrees of poverty. "Absolute poverty" is defined as being in dire need of the basics of life—food, clothing, and housing—but it is only the people in the top third of the urban income scale who are able to live in relative comfort. A case might therefore be made for designing development projects for persons in the lower two-thirds of a city's population, those not able to compete advantageously as consumers or producers in their own economies. Even a more conservative cutoff at the median income level would leave roughly half a million persons in Guayaquil and La Paz as potential targets for development programs. In such a large agglomeration, there are apt to be many subgroups with different cultural preferences and values. These cultural distinctions often determine whether a family or community wants a particular type of benefit offered by a project. Like the subgroups of renters, women, and youths, these cultural subgroups among the poor are often little understood by project planners and managers. The problem again is not the indifference of project staff but their perspective. A few examples from the two projects illustrate the importance of some of these cultures of poverty.

Urbanism and infrastructure. San Antonio in La Paz was one of the five communities referred to at the outset of this chapter that rejected upgrading when it was first offered by the municipality. One reason for this, as mentioned, was political. Another reason was discovered by my assistant

Yolanda Barriga during the three months she lived in San Antonio. Many of the people of that barrio had come to La Paz from rural areas, where they had not had water or sewerage in their houses. These recent immigrants were not accustomed to urban amenities and simply did not value them. In contrast, the people of 8 de Diciembre had spent most or all of their lives in the city. This urbanism, as well as the proclivities of the nonpartisan, middle-class leadership, helped explain why piped-in water and sewer systems were valued in 8 de Diciembre but not in San Antonio.

Class and housing. As shown in chapter 4, the piso-techo core houses in Floresta, Guayaquil, were not as catalytic as expected because almost half of the families selected to live in them did not have access to the capital to finish the units as they wanted to before moving in. Their income and savings were insufficient and few people had relatives who would lend them money for such purposes.

Another, far less tangible constraint appeared to be one of values. Half of the owners of the piso-techo units (53 out of 104) had moved in within the first five months. Although they may have had access to more money, that was not the only reason they were able to move in. Many of this first group were able to pay for finishing their houses because they were willing to use cheap materials. They did generally complete the outer walls with the same cement block or brick used to construct the core house, but they often created inner partitions from inexpensive, makeshift material such as sheets hung from lines. This was only a temporary arrangement until they could afford to complete their houses as they wished. The occupant of one such partially built structure remarked, "We're happy to live this way; we'll improve the house with time, when we have the money. Some of these others," and he gestured to several of the unoccupied structures, "they'll wait where they are until they can afford to build the little palaces of their dreams. I don't understand those people." Even within the same income group people reacted differently to unfinished housing partly because of their varying standards and perceptions of what was acceptable (see chapter 4).

This discrepancy in preferences between persons of the same general income was especially pronounced with regard to type of housing and infrastructure. Most of the poor of Guayaquil live in houses made of bamboo, which is very inexpensive. It is also well suited to the hot, tropical climate: houses made of bamboo are far better ventilated than the ones made of concrete or brick. Bamboo does present a fire hazard, but there is an inexpensive treatment that makes the material fire-resistant. While living in my own hot, poorly ventilated, small house with concrete slab walls in Floresta, so close to the thousands of bamboo houses of Guasmo, I often thought it ironic that we in the government housing project were paying a lot more for our living quarters than the people in Guasmo, but they lived in far greater comfort (though of course without the services).

During my many conversations with people living in bamboo housing in informal settlements, in downtown rental quarters, and in the concrete and brick project housing of Floresta, I became aware of two submarkets among the poor of Guayaquil, each aspiring to different living environments. One gave priority to infrastructure, while the other stressed durable building materials. The two groups were divided as much by cultural values and orientation as by income. My previous participant-observation experiences in other Latin American cities, particularly in Rio de Janeiro, made me believe that this division was not unique to Guayaquil but existed in other urban areas of the continent. These market differences in values, as well as income, could usefully be taken into account in urban projects.[3]

One articulate older woman in Guasmo who was active in community affairs represented one point of view. When I mentioned that I lived in the neighboring housing project of Floresta, she looked at me quizzically, saying "I don't know what people see in those government projects. This house is bigger and the bamboo allows it to be far better ventilated. The materials of houses in La Floresta are not right for our climate. I have a daughter who lives in one of the government projects [with houses similar to those in Floresta]; whenever I visit her, I want to leave right away. Those houses are too hot and stuffy." She proceeded to say that many people favored the poorly ventilated cement and brick houses because they conferred status. The social stigma of bamboo this dark-complexioned woman compared to the prejudice against tightly curled or "kinky" hair. She believed that the people of Guayaquil were largely from the countryside, where they had lived in bamboo houses. Bamboo is what they were used to and still wanted. She did, however, value the water and sewerage facilities of Floresta. And on hearing of the sites-and-services concept, she expressed the opinion that it would be beneficial for the low-income persons of Guayaquil.[4]

A number of my neighbors in Floresta and others who planned to move there expressed a very different opinion. Although the consensus was that the best feature of the government project was ownership of home and land, there were favorable comments on the type of housing as well. "Floresta is a good place to live; the houses here are made of good, solid material." These comments came particularly from persons such as teachers and nurses whose status was higher than indicated by their earnings. They were perhaps therefore anxious to confirm their higher status with the more prestigious cement or brick as opposed to the bamboo of the poor and the countryside. These professionals also generally came from downtown apartments. Truck drivers and manual laborers in bamboo housing in Guasmo did not attribute the same value to durable housing materials. In view of the failure of the piso-techo experiment, the thousands of persons living in unserviced squatter areas, and the considerable expenditure on building and managing housing projects such as Floresta, it seems that an appreciation of the various cultures of urban poverty would help to achieve an appropriate match between project design and beneficiary.

It would not be expensive or time-consuming to conduct a series of conversational interviews in selected low-income areas during the design phase of a project. It might be useful to have a participant observer live in an area for two or three months. The aim of this investigation would be to ascertain not only the people's income and ability to pay but also their values with regard to shelter and infrastructure. The design and promotion of the project would take account of the population groups that had been identified according to income and values. This would avoid the piso-techo situation in which there was a mismatch between people's ability to pay and the housing standards they desired. Subtle class distinctions regarding housing choice are best understood during project preparation through open, guided, yet flexible techniques of interviewing, which allow people to express not only who they are but also what they value.

Lessons

In late 1984 the *Washington Post* ran a three-part series, "Africa: The Hungry Continent." The second article reviewed the very unhappy aid experiences in Tanzania, which has received more foreign assistance since 1970 than any other African nation—a total of more than $2 billion. Aid grew in size from $51 million in 1970 to $625 million a decade later, when it represented two-thirds of Tanzania's development budget. Some 90 percent of Tanzania's population are farmers. Much of the aid went for the purchase of modern equipment, which quickly fell into disrepair. The article reported that "per capita food production during that decade (1970–1980) has fallen 12 percent." Since 1979 Tanzania has become "dependent on food handouts for survival." The *Post* article quotes an aide to President Nyerere of Tanzania, who admitted, "It's our fault at least as much as the donors' because, after all, we agreed to their projects."[5]

Many issues come together to explain the problems of foreign assistance in Tanzania, from droughts to falling world prices of farm products, to management of parastatals and dislocation caused by the villagization program. Stephen Gurman of Canadian University Services Overseas pointed to the insufficient appreciation of the context of the peasant village on the part of program designers and managers. "Few donors were equipped to ascertain what peasants really might want or need. It's not very pleasant to spend a month in a peasant village, so people tend to do a lot of their program development from offices in Dar," he said. "They take a quick field trip and pass through villages in a cloud of dust. A lot of important little details can get ignored."

The lesson is the same in the projects discussed in this book: the effective project designer and manager, in person or through the eyes and ears of others, must be there with the people he wants to help for enough time to know what they feel, what they think, and what they do in relation to the project.

The successful implementing agencies in the two projects observed were learning this lesson. In Guayaquil, the Housing Bank resolved to reach low-income borrowers and reduce late payments in their home improvement loan program by sending urban extension workers into the slums where the borrowers lived. These extensionists were to help the borrowers and potential borrowers understand how the program worked by explaining both benefits and repayment obligations. In La Paz my co-worker living in San Antonio found that the municipality's executing unit had instituted an effective outreach system known as the *hormiga* (ant). Social workers made door-to-door visits to find out the concerns of the residents and to explain the program to them in nontechnical language.

In the two projects reviewed here the most successful components were the ones that best appreciated the local context: the credit programs for small businesses and home improvement and the upgrading program for the homeowners in 8 de Diciembre. They were planned for the right people in the right places at the right time. The proper contextual alignment of projects and people is maintained by respecting the people not as passive beneficiaries but as active users of what a project has to offer.

In many development projects, like the two discussed here, people pay for what they receive. Cost recovery is a central tenet of World Bank urban projects, because cost recovery makes it possible to replicate these efforts on a much larger scale with domestic resources. Yet very often development projects continue to approach the people not as paying clients but as beneficiaries who should naturally be grateful for anything they receive. My neighbors in 8 de Diciembre were very firm when they told me, "We have a right to expect improvements that meet our needs. We are paying for this project." Public housing projects in developing countries are notorious for having problems with the collection of monthly payments. The more involved these people are with the projects, not as passive beneficiaries but as customers to be served, and the more they are listened to, the more likely they are to meet their payment obligations. Listening to the people is not only what one might expect of professionals concerned with development, it also makes economic sense.

« »

In roughly a year and a half it was shown that, by living with and otherwise getting to know project beneficiaries, an experienced observer may gain insights useful for improving a project. Participant observation and related techniques, qualitative and quantitative, appeared to be an effective management tool for international development work. The question was whether the approach could have a wide application elsewhere. To be transferable it would need to be carried out largely by persons from the countries undergoing development. Part II describes this next step, in which the approach was transferred to other areas and the participant-observer evaluations were done by local practitioners.

« PART II »

Helping Others Listen

« **6** »

THE CHALLENGE OF TRANSFERABILITY

In August 1984, with some trepidation, I traveled to Natal, a peaceful state capital in the Northeast of Brazil. It was my third visit to train and supervise local project personnel in the methods of participant-observer evaluation. Since February, participant observers had been residing in a village of artisans in the interior, and in a community of fishermen on the coast. I was now to hear the results of the observers' studies, which had been completed and assimilated by project management. My anxiety was unfounded: both evaluations had been well received by management. The fishing village offered a telling and representative demonstration of the efficacy of this approach.

After more than two years of existence, a fishing cooperative in the state of Rio Grande do Norte had attracted only about 10 percent of the fishermen for whom it was intended. To attempt to determine why, World Bank project officers and local management had agreed to try out the participant-observer evaluation method, using host-country observers. Project officials selected Luiz Kmentt, a young man in his mid-twenties who had recently received a university degree in economics, as the observer. He was to live in two fishing communities for several weeks each and spend an additional few weeks in and around the central cooperative in the state capital of Natal. After almost three months in these three areas living with and talking to fishermen, Kmentt made the following observations about the role of local fish buyers ("intermediaries") in the project:

> The fishermen are less exploited if they deal with the cooperative, yet none of them are conscious of this, owing to the anticooperative cam-

paign carried out by the intermediaries. The majority of the active [cooperative] members are not individuals who are conscious of the advantages of cooperativism but fishermen who do not get along well with the intermediaries. On the other hand, many nonmembers give preference to the intermediaries in order to maintain ties of family or friendship.

There exists misinformation about the actual prices [offered by the cooperative for fish] such that none of the nonmember fishermen can say exactly what this price is. The notion that the fishermen have . . . is that the price is lower than what the intermediary pays, whereas the price of the cooperative is 20 percent higher than the price of the intermediaries. This error is daily reinforced by the intermediaries. The anticooperative mentality is such that the fishermen do not believe that the cooperative is paying a higher price when they are informed that this is indeed the case.[1]

The local manager of this Bank-supported fishing cooperative said that she learned more about the intermediaries from this participant-observer evaluation than she had known in the four years she had been involved with this project. As a result of information from the participant observer, she instituted a comprehensive new promotional campaign to educate the fishermen about cooperativism, took steps to replace a cooperative administrator seen by the fishermen as cold and uncommunicative, and redistributed profits to the fishermen, thus redressing one of their major grievances.

The Second Generation of Participant Observation

After my visit to Natal, I knew that the success of the participant-observer evaluation method was real. It was not tied to the particular circumstances of La Paz or Guayaquil, nor, as some observers had suggested, was it dependent on my own direct participation. The participant-observer evaluations in Natal on artisan's and fishermen's cooperatives had demonstrated that the approach could be transferred. Local people within developing countries could usefully listen to their own compatriots and thereby contribute to their own country's development process.

An outcome of the initial evaluation work in La Paz and Guayaquil was that the World Bank decided to transfer the approach to urban projects in Brazil and Thailand and rural projects in the Altiplano of Bolivia. This time the evaluations were to be done by local personnel; the Bank would provide only training. This second generation of participant-observer evaluations was to address a number of questions posed by Bank staff: How much is the success of this approach wed to a particular individual? Can persons be found in developing countries who are both qualified and willing to undertake this kind of evaluation? Would host-country nationals, who had the status related to university training, be averse to living and associating closely with persons of lower income and social position? How would local managers react to this approach? Would they think that they already knew enough about project beneficiaries and that this kind of intense involvement represented an unwelcome and possibly damaging intrusion? What value would findings from this kind of evaluation have for host-country and Bank management? Finally, what are the costs and administrative requirements of setting up and monitoring participant-observer evaluation?

Diverse settings were chosen for this experiment: Bangkok, the capital of Thailand, and Recife, the major urban center of Brazil's impoverished Northeast; three medium-size cities (of approximately 100,000 population each), Chiang Mai in northern Thailand, Natal in Brazil's Northeast, and Florianópolis in the developed southern part of Brazil; and forty-one rural communities in the Bolivian highland provinces of Ingavi, Omasuyos, Los Andes, and Ulla Ulla. The project components evaluated included agriculture and wool production, slum upgrading and low-cost housing, and employment generation through artisan, milk, and fishing cooperatives (see tables 5 and 6).

Table 5. Second Generation Participant-Observer Evaluations

Country	City	Project component	Evaluation methodology
Brazil	Natal	Artisan cooperative	Participant observation (PO)
		Fishing cooperative	PO
	Recife	Slum relocation	Qualitative interviewing (QI)
		Slum upgrading	PO, QI
		Fishing cooperative	PO, QI
	Florianópolis	Milk cooperative	QI, Institutional assessment
		Fishing cooperative	PO
		Washerwomen's Association	QI, PO
Bolivia	Villa Ulla	Wool production	QI, PO
	Ingavi	Agriculture	QI, PO
	Los Andes	Agriculture	QI, PO
Thailand	Bangkok	Low-cost housing	QI, PO
		Slum relocation	QI
	Chiang Mai	Low-cost housing	PO, QI

Table 6. Local Cost of Participant-Observer Evaluation and Amount
of Project Loan, by Country
(1984 U.S. dollars)

Country	Number of projects	Local cost	Amount of project loan[a]
Brazil	2	30,000	17,000,000
Bolivia	3	7,000	36,500,000
Thailand	2	14,000	10,500,000
Total	7	51,000	64,000,000

a. Refers to portion of project evaluated.

Evaluations were done by host-country nationals at minimal cost. With few exceptions, evaluators were recruited locally and hired as consultants.[2] Most were trained at the university level in the social sciences—economics, sociology, anthropology, agronomy, education, or social work. All had previous experience in research among low-income persons, but none had used qualitative methods for the purpose of project evaluation before.

Evaluations were conducted in four to six months and local costs averaged $7,000 per project—a small amount for projects with an average cost of $9 million. The methods adopted in each country were primarily qualitative interview surveys and participant observation with case studies, which are the two main tools of operational evaluations. Evaluators were given little initial training. Where possible they received guidance during the fieldwork, which helped them to blend qualitative methods and quantitative representation and to focus inquiries on areas of concern to management.

In Brazil, where participant-observer evaluation was conducted more extensively than anywhere else during this second phase, the experience is instructive. Eight diverse components were evaluated by fourteen local consultants in three cities (see table 5) in the course of a year. The average length of time required to evaluate each project component was three months. Evaluators spent a total of forty-eight person-months conducting the evaluations. Supervision time by local implementation offices was one-quarter the evaluation time, or twelve months. My own time spent on orientation was one-quarter of the local supervision time, three months, spread over three trips, to introduce the approach at the outset, monitor ongoing work midway, and assist with the preparation and review of final reports at the year's end. The cost breakdown for these diverse functions was roughly $24,000 for the evaluator-consultants, $6,000 for local supervision, and $18,000 for Bank guidance, exclusive of travel. The costs for both supervision and guidance will come down markedly after the initial experimental phase.

Assistance to Management

The consensus of operational management staff, both at the Bank and in the three countries where this approach was tested, was that participant-observer evaluation increased the ability of management to improve project performance. The chief of evaluation of FIDEM, one of the principal participating host-country institutions in Recife, categorized the contributions of participant-observer evaluation as follows:

- Ratification. The findings of the evaluation confirm the significance of one feature of a project.
- Correction. The evaluation provides information that can lead to modifications in the way the project is executed.
- New insights. The evaluation sheds light on a hitherto unknown or little-known aspect of the beneficiary community that helps the project be executed more smoothly.

Ratification. Recife provided two examples of confirmation of a significant element. The first concerned plans to establish a cooperative in Brasilia Teimosa, a poor fishing community. The fishermen expressed strong support for the idea of a cooperative, primarily to ensure good prices for their catch, provide ice for storage, and serve as a source of credit for expenses. Knowledge of their commitment to the cooperative concept was most useful to the municipality's executing agency, which had to defend the project before the new mayor, who wanted to replace the cooperative with a state enterprise.

The second example concerned one component of a slum upgrading project. The same mayor, elected after project negotiations were completed, felt little identification with the project. He wanted to eliminate the drainage component of the upgrading program because he thought it an expensive, time-consuming activity that was largely invisible and would be of little immediate political benefit to him. The participant observer who lived in the upgrading area for three months and his two co-evaluators who visited it daily reported that drainage was a high priority for the people of the area. Water seeped into their land and houses, and they were anxious to get rid of it. This evidence convinced the mayor to retain the drainage component in the project.

Participant-observer evaluation may also ratify negative results. Its findings may confirm managers' hunches that a project is not appropriate for particular people in a particular locale. The research team that spent time with beneficiaries of three World Bank rural projects in the Bolivian Altiplano produced information to this effect. The team members, who spoke the indigenous Aymara, lived and had intensive discussions with the highland Indians for four months. They concluded that the projects had done little to benefit the people beyond providing subsidized fertilizer, which was used to increase potato production. It was clear from the Indians' own words that some of the projects' main objectives—providing technical assistance, reaching the poorer farmers, and improving agricultural technology— were not achieved, primarily because of poor communication between beneficiaries and project extension agents. The cultural and historical contexts of these Altiplano projects required close and intensive interaction between agents and beneficiaries for the project's success. Such interaction may not have been feasible, however, given the dual nature of Bolivian society (Indian-Spanish), the difficulty of recruiting competent technical persons with adequate linguistic and cross-cultural skills, and the severe economic crisis through which Bolivia was passing. For the World Bank program staff who had commissioned this evaluation, the findings confirmed their own opinions regarding the need for change in the kind of projects the Bank supports in this poorly understood region of South America.

Correction. In Recife—as in every other place where participant observation has been carried out—an important finding was that beneficiaries simply did not understand key aspects of the projects that had been designed for them. In the Capibaribe Valley, where the project was relocating certain small, low-income communities to new and better housing, the people being relocated were confused about where they were to go and the people in communities undergoing upgrading were unsure whether they would lose their residences in the process. The municipal executing agency had been relying on its own district offices on or near project sites to disseminate information about the project. From in-depth discussion with residents of these areas by one participant observer and four interviewers it was clear that these municipal outposts, despite their strategic location, were not getting the message to the people. Public officials in the branch offices expected residents to come to them if they had questions; information was transmitted directly only to community "leaders," who were either unknown or, in most cases, not respected by the people they were supposed to represent. The situation was reminiscent of that in Guasmo Norte in Guayaquil. On the basis of the information gathered by the operational evaluation in Recife, the project unit began to deal directly with residents through group meetings and the door-to-door distribution of written bulletins.

In Thailand, participant-observer evaluation is contributing to an important change in housing policy. As stated in chapter 4, the evaluation found that low-income persons believed unfinished core housing was inferior to completed units which could be occupied immediately. The unfinished core unit provided by the project was a mere 21 square meters, too small for the average family of five or six persons. Typically, completing and extending the unit cost nine times the average monthly income of residents in housing sites in Bangkok and Chiang Mai. The absence of capital for needed construction appeared to inhibit many people from moving to the site as early as expected. After fifteen to eighteen months 50 percent of the purchased, unfinished units at Nong Hoy in Chiang Mai and 25 percent of those at Tung Song Hong in Bangkok were still unoccupied. The need to pay for finishing the units may have kept the project from reaching the low-income population for which it was intended. Half of the buyers of the least expensive units had incomes above the cutoff line that had been set as a criterion. The results in Thailand, which were similar to those in Ecuador, suggest that reducing the physical dimensions of the housing unit sold may not resolve the difficulties faced by low-income persons as much as expected. Although people do often choose to complete their homes gradually, they place a value on houses they can live in right away. People also seem to prefer to use materials of the same quality used in the first stage of construction and found in neighboring houses. Partly as a result of these evaluation findings, the Thai government is returning to the concept of providing complete though small residential structures, ready for immediate occupancy, combined with increased access to credit for home expansion.

New insights. In Recife the evaluators found among the poor an unexpected value for health and sanitation, often considered largely middle-class priorities. The people in the upgrading area recognized the need for better latrines and were willing to pay a modest amount for these improvements despite their low incomes (averaging roughly $90 a month). This finding indicated that cost recovery for this component was indeed feasible, despite objections by some local politicians. In the same upgrading area evaluators discovered that an old monument—a *cruzeiro*, or cross—was the source of community pride. The project unit incorporated the restoration of this monument into the upgrading work and thereby won support among community members who had previously been lukewarm about the project.

Other new insights were provided when participant observers uncovered diverse strata of low-income workers that had not previously been apparent. The evaluation team in the fishing community in Recife found that one class of fishermen, mostly women, did not use boats at all—a departure from the executing agency's concept of how fishing was being done. These persons, generally the poorest in the community, earned their livelihood by raking shrimp, prawns, crabs, and snails from the rivers and mudflats. Their concern was primarily for a guaranteed market for their perishable commodity rather than for the fair and stable prices sought by the more affluent seagoing fishermen. Enlightened by this finding, project management could encourage the cooperative to attend to the different needs of each fishing subgroup.

North of Recife, in Rio Grande do Norte, the participant observer who lived among artisans and handicraft workers revealed the frozen inferior status of one category of artisans, tranceiras, who braid hemp into cords which the more privileged pieceworkers use to produce a final product. The braiders receive roughly one-third the income of the pieceworkers, who themselves seldom exceed the minimum monthly wage of 50,256 cruzeiros, or $42. The braiders naturally want to become pieceworkers but find it most difficult to do so. This is partly because the cooperative provides credit to pieceworkers for sewing machines and eyeglasses (this kind of detailed work taxes the eyes) but not to braiders. Learning of this vast difference in income and opportunity between the two artisan groups, the project manager set in motion policies to train braiders and provide them credit for sewing machines. As a first step, the manager prevailed on the state agency that supplies low-cost eyeglasses to pieceworkers to extend the same privileges to braiders.

Acceptance by Managers

Most of the managers who have witnessed participant-observer evaluations have become enthusiastic supporters of the approach. In several cases their conversion has been a pronounced shift in attitude. All but two of the managers whose projects underwent this intensive review had been mildly supportive of the approach at the outset. Many, however, appeared to accept the idea more because the World Bank and persons of higher authority were favorable to it than because of their own personal conviction. Two managers opposed the approach and were overridden by their superiors. One of them, the Recife project manager, stated unequivocally, "Having someone live in the project site can only get in the way of project execution. I see no benefits in this approach." After the Recife evaluation team had spent three months among the low-income beneficiaries of the project and submitted its final report, this same project manager stated, "I have been involved with many development projects, but I have never had such helpful feedback. I now want this evaluation approach to expand so as to reach beneficiaries wherever we have project activities."

In Natal, the project manager had made a similar though less complete turnaround. At the outset she had approached the experiment with an open mind but had been anxious not to spend more than $1,000 for each of the two participant observers employed. She seemed skeptical about what she would learn from people who lived in project areas, although she did give serious thought to the topics for informal interviews. She (like other project managers) realized there were important issues involving the beneficiaries' attitudes and behavior about which she had little information. She was willing to give the evaluation experiment a try, but clearly did not expect much benefit from it. Upon completion of the evaluation with artisan and fishing cooperatives, she said she would now have participant observers evaluate ten of the sixteen components (all of those that were oriented to people) in the Bank-supported project over which she had responsibility. She felt the benefits gained from this intensive evaluation far outweighed the costs.

Once results began to come in, the approach appealed to managers at all levels as a simple way of providing feedback to decisionmakers. Project managers directly responsible for day-to-day implementation saw the most immediate benefits. In Brazil, as in the initial experiment in Bolivia and Ecuador, support for participant-observer evaluation extended with few exceptions to state officials and ministers of the central government. The one or two managers who questioned the approach appeared to do so not out of dissatisfaction with any intrinsic aspects of it, but out of concern that information produced might be used to undermine their own authority or jeopardize the program for which they were responsible. At the federal level, the National Urban Development Council (CNDU) of the Ministry of Interior of Brazil judged this approach to have sufficient merit to warrant institutionalization throughout all the municipalities in which it sponsored development activities.

Assessment

Managers appreciate hearing from people whose lives they are affecting. Business managers receive feedback from consumers through the marketplace. Development administrators do not have a marketplace for their "products," which are often supplied to consumer-beneficiaries with little attention to demand. Managers of development programs realize, however, that the way beneficiaries use a project is critical to its success or failure as a developmental endeavor. In the projects evaluated operationally in Bolivia, Brazil, and Thailand, project managers and, to an even greater degree, World Bank officials were extremely distant from the beneficiaries and had little awareness of how they were reacting. The officials therefore welcomed participant-observer evaluation as a tool to help bridge the gap between administrators and project beneficiaries. They saw this approach as providing information which was useful not only for making constant improvements in the project but also for indicating the effects of the project.

One of the initial difficulties in developing the participant-observer evaluation approach in Brazil was the confusion between it and impact evaluation. The Brazilian implementation institutions had previously been trying to conduct traditional impact assessments, establishing base-line indicators (of health, income, literacy, and so on) against which to measure changes produced by the project, yet wondering whether the project would in fact make significant and measurable differences in these areas. At a meeting to discuss the value of both the findings and the overall approach, a top official from SUDENE, the principal government entity overseeing development in the Northeast, remarked that there was no need for a separate impact evaluation. The principal factors needed to assess the project's worth—percentages of fishermen belonging to a cooperative, prices received from the cooperative compared with those from intermediaries, payment for and satisfaction with latrines in an upgrading project, and so on—could be collected at various times by using a combination of the participant-observer and qualitative interviewing techniques employed in the evaluation. To assess impact one would simply need to look at the changes in these indicators over time. These periodic soundings would also serve the immediate needs of management by providing feedback for the ongoing improvement of the project. Separate impact evaluations were seen as warranted only when there is interest in (and the possibility of) attributing to projects the changes in, for instance, the income or health of beneficiaries. Given the difficulty of establishing causality, however, and the constant need for useful and timely information for management purposes, it was recommended that local development institutions place emphasis on participant-observer evaluation.

The shortcomings of the participant-observer evaluations in Bolivia, Brazil, and Thailand were mostly because of the inexperience of practitioners and supervisors. The two biggest problems, as reflected in the reports, were inadequate analysis and substantiation. In many evaluations, findings were presented as raw data, without the analysis that would reveal their operational significance. For instance, the evaluation of a slum removal project in Recife discussed the lack of respect for local leaders among beneficiaries without addressing the manner in which leaders were selected. A report from Bangkok recommended community organization without specifying concrete issues around which such organization might take place. There was also a pervasive tendency throughout the reporting to present findings in an anecdotal or purely descriptive fashion without the necessary factual substantiation from quantitative analysis. The stress on qualitative understanding inadvertently understated the importance of quantitative representation. Often opinions were attributed to beneficiary groups with no indication of how widely they were shared.

A third problem, which helped explain the other two, arose from the incomplete understanding of the approach by project managers, who underestimated both the difficulty of execution and the value of findings. There is a need to refine the orientation process so that managers will not only see the benefits of the approach but also be able to administer it effectively.

Proceeding to Future Generations of Listeners

Participant-observer evaluation is attractive to project managers because they are able to see it as serving their interests. Unlike many kinds of evaluation, which managers often understandably see as judgmental and threatening, this approach is conceived as a tool for improving project performance. Few managers deny the need for better and more timely feedback from the people whose lives they are trying to improve, and they were particularly receptive to the approach when

- They had questions about behavioral factors related to a successful or problematic aspect of a project. The use of participant observers in fishing communities to discover why so few fishermen joined cooperatives sponsored by the project is one example. Another is the artisan cooperative in Rio Grande do Norte, where one community was producing excellent items in vast quantities while other communities were either mediocre or poor in one or both respects. Here the participant observer spent time in communities representing the range of production, from excellent to poor, to understand what factors accounted for the differences.

- The approach coincided with a political democratization process. Both Bolivia and Brazil were moving from authoritarian to more open, participatory forms of government during the execution of these evaluations. Political leaders saw a congruence between this operational, human inquiry and their own efforts to fashion programs responsive to people's needs and wants.

- Projects had intangible goals that were not susceptible to conventional statistical analysis. While in the Northeast of Brazil I discussed this approach with managers of a World Bank–supported rural development project that placed great emphasis on fostering popular participation and individual initiative. Project administrators saw participant-observer evaluation as an appropriate method to determine the nature and extent of participation in the program.

Consistent with serving the interests of managers, the approach gives them control over both the selection of evaluators and the dissemination of findings from the evaluation. Despite the disarming simplicity of the concept, the evaluators, especially those engaged in participant observation, need to be selected with care so as not to impair the execution of the approach. The attributes of a good evaluator are not derived from specialization in any particular academic discipline. The good qualitative interviewer or participant observer ideally combines several qualities:

- Experience with management or operations of a development activity
- Familiarity with basic social research methods and rudimentary statistical analysis
- Sufficient maturity to discern the relevance of what is observed
- Openness to others and a capacity to learn from listening
- Ability to relate well to persons regardless of status.

Experience in Latin America and Asia has shown that there is a large reservoir of qualified candidates for participant-observer evaluation. Contrary to the dire predictions of some development professionals, competent individuals were found in little time to carry out qualitative interviews and be participant observers in each of the four experimental countries, Bolivia, Brazil, Ecuador, and Thailand. These persons combined analytical skills with facility in interpersonal relations. As recently as twenty years ago most university graduates in rigidly stratified societies such as many of those in Latin America might have been reluctant to spend much time with the poor, but many of the present generation of graduates saw the experience of sharing lifestyles with less fortunate members of their own societies as a desirable opportunity to bridge a social and economic gap. From all indications, the number of individuals with the commitment and skill to do this kind of person-to-person evaluation will increase in the future.

The importance of experience and mature judgment should not be underestimated in choosing participant-observer evaluators. Because of the apparent simplicity of the work involved—spending time and informally conversing with low-income folk—and because of the discomfort associated with such an endeavor, however, it was felt that the job of participant-observer evaluator was better left to the young. On the one hand, people in their twenties or early thirties are also more apt to be free of familial or occupational attachments that would prevent them from dislocating their lives to spend intensive periods with project beneficiaries. Young persons are less apt to raise suspicions than are more senior individuals. On the other hand, the primary ingredient of a good participant-observer evaluator is judgment. He or she needs to know when to ask what of whom. It is important for the evaluator to know something about representative sampling. It is even more important for the evaluator to know how to gain the confidence of people with whom he or she is conversing. But it is essential that the evaluator know what kinds of issues to pursue because of their utility for project improvement. The power to discern what is germane to the goals of the project comes from experience with other development efforts, with research, and with operations. Although much of the information collected will be useful because of its source, the "people," the best insights will come from mature, experienced observers.

Participant-observer evaluation needs good monitoring; intensive scrutiny should alternate with periods of detachment. The evaluator initially spends a brief familiarization period at the office of the project implementing staff. Once out in the community, however, the evaluator needs to be left alone for the entry phase of interviewing or participant observation. Usually within the first month a monitor, generally from the evaluation staff of the implementing agency, should visit or be contacted. There may be reason for some interaction to take place away from the site of the observation to avoid arousing suspicion. The monitoring should proceed periodically throughout the execution of the evaluation and should encompass:

- The soundness of the methodology employed. Two evaluators in Chiang Mai had been poorly instructed in the approach by an official of a government institution in Bangkok. They had delivered written questionnaires to respondents under the doors of their houses. Monitoring corrected this error so that informal interviews and participant observation involving on-site residence became the dominant modes of inquiry.

- The relevance of information to management concerns. One misguided but very earnest evaluator in Bolivia spent almost two months doing intensive interviews to develop individual life histories, which, while rich in detail and interesting in themselves, had little or nothing to do with the project being evaluated.
- Acceptance of the evaluator by the beneficiaries. One local researcher lived with a resident couple in one of the urban projects being evaluated. On my return to the area I learned that, although the assistant had made close personal ties to several of the neighbors, she had provoked hostility from the young woman of the household. The reason was simple: the assistant had criticized the woman's housekeeping to the latter's mother-in-law, behind her back.

« »

A prime indicator of the success of this experiment with participant-observer evaluation will be whether development agencies adopt it as part of their normal operations. In Brazil and Thailand, where participant observation and qualitative interviewing were first carried out under the auspices of local project implementing institutions, managers have said that they will take the next step toward institutionalization and continue this approach with their own funding.

As with any institutional effort, adoption of the new approach requires appropriate staffing. Given the profound departure from traditional methods, considerable changes may be needed in the kind of persons overseeing and conducting evaluation. Participant-observer evaluation relies on the evaluator's ability to listen and to recognize the utility of issues arising in a particular context rather than on preformulated questionnaires or sophisticated statistical analysis. The skills needed are far more anthropological in method and managerial in substance than those now practiced by most evaluators. Institutionalization of the method within a development agency will require management support, senior professionals experienced with this approach, and a network of consultants able to carry it out. Eventually the approach must be accepted by all operational staff so as to ensure its inclusion as an integral part of all projects that rely on people as the subjects of their own development.

« 7 »

PRECEPTS FOR PARTICIPANT-OBSERVER EVALUATION

The little girl was crying. She was standing in the dusty road under the hot midday sun of the Bolivian Altiplano. A man selling ice cream was passing by. The girl's parents, sitting on the hillside of the settlement of 8 de Diciembre, had just told her they didn't have the money to buy any ice cream. On impulse I provided the few pesos necessary to fill that out-stretched little hand with the ice cream it so avidly sought. (The amount of money needed was not so large as to offend the family by the disparity in resources between myself and them.) In an instant the little girl's face became all smiles and her father asked me if I would join them on the side of the hill.

The purchase of ice cream for a small child led to a friendship with her parents and grandmother. This marked the beginning of my contact with the neighborhood's renters. I had by this time been living in 8 de Diciembre for close to a month and was starting to realize that renters were benefiting from the project in quite different ways from the homeowners. I guessed that the parents might be renters because they were sitting near the houses where I had been told renters lived. Over the following few months I was to get to know all three generations of this family quite well. The man and his wife had been sitting in front of his mother's rented house. They lived in rented rooms in another part of the neighborhood. Over the remainder of my time in the barrio, these and other personal contacts helped provide an understanding of rental conditions that allowed me to formulate topics for later, more structured interviews with a representative sample of 8 de Diciembre residents.

The anecdote illustrates the central tenet of the hybrid of methods and techniques I have called participant-observer evaluation: understanding conditions in an area where a development project is under way requires close personal contact and open, conversational interviews in an atmosphere of mutual confidence. The inclusion of "participant-observer" in the name given to this evaluation emphasizes the other-directedness of the approach: an open, listening stance, critical yet empathetic, is taken in a social setting by an observer who has been referred to as a "professional"—and I would add friendly—"stranger."[1]

Participant-observation evaluation as used in this book is an inclusive, general term which "involves some amount of genuinely social intervention in the field with the subjects of the study [or evaluation], some direct observation of relevant events, some formal and a great deal of informal interviewing, some systematic counting, some collection of documents . . . and open-endedness in the direction the study takes."[2] Findings are sought and organized so that wherever possible they may be quantified. In this way, the insights derived through open, qualitative exploration are given concrete form in numbers. The description of participant-observer evaluation draws heavily on the experience of evaluating the two urban development projects in La Paz and Guayaquil. Eight project components in the two cities were evaluated with varying forms of the general, inclusive, and participatory approach.

Participant-observer evaluation, changing as it does to meet the particular needs of a particular project component, does not lend itself to precise cookbook formulation. A brief list of steps to take in conducting participant-observer evaluation with on-site residence is presented in appendix A to this book. Practitioners of development projects may use the following premises and precepts as guidelines for fashioning their own participant-observer evaluation to meet the needs of a specific situation.

The primary objective of participant-observer evaluation is to provide project managers with useful and timely information to help them make decisions that will improve the project's performance. A second objective is to elicit contributions from beneficiaries to policy formulation. Third, this approach should generate insights and findings that, while preliminary, can serve as hypotheses for more rigorous research.

Participant-observer evaluation is eclectic, responsive, and flexible. It is intended to serve management rather than to stand in judgment. The approach proceeds from the following premises about development and development institutions.

- Most development projects are experimental. They need information to help them evolve, but they are too new to be useful arenas for testing hypotheses using predetermined variables.

- In addition to the routine yet important monitoring of a project's physical and financial progress, the manager of a project that has social content needs to understand its sociocultural environment. The history of a place and its people, their traditions, values, and forms of organization are essential ingredients for effective development work.

- Understanding the sociocultural milieu in which a project is to operate is far more a matter of stance, or approach, than of time or cost. Listening is the prescribed mode.

- Generally, development institutions are inadequately staffed to be as attentive to beneficiaries' views as they need to be.

The kind of information which the development community needs about projects defies traditional categories of learning; it is both qualitative and quantitative. Participant-observer evaluation is based on the observation techniques of social anthropology but draws as well on a variety of other social sciences, particularly psychology and sociology, and on innate common sense and intuition. Inasmuch as participant-observer evaluation is directed to decisionmaking, it is also related to the theory and practice of management and administration.

Although development projects are often experimental they are not set in laboratory conditions. Given the difficulties of controlling variables, assigning causality to the project rather than to external factors, and selecting valid control groups, there is widespread disenchantment with the use of experimental or quasi-experimental design in the evaluation of projects that introduce social change.[3] In many development projects not only are conditions not propitious for scientific testing but the socioeconomic context is too little known to warrant the elaboration of useful hypotheses. Development, the enhancement of an individual's potential for self-fulfillment, takes place over time. This process is not predictable. Nor is it ever adequately understood on the basis of abstractions; it must be experienced to be fully understood. Since most designers, planners, and supervisors of development activities do not directly experience these activities as beneficiaries, it is important that they seek the understanding of persons whose business it is to do this type of learning. The following are the basic precepts for the practitioners of participant-observer evaluation.

1. Know the Setting

The development project is best appreciated as part of the larger society and economy in which it is located. The project is the creation of institutions, national and international, and particularly of certain key individuals within those institutions. The first step of a participant-observer is to become familiar with the terrain—physical, socioeconomic, and institutional. This entails

- Spending time at the executing agency, digesting project documents, and getting to know implementation staff
- Reading the relevant literature on the area, the people, and the sector
- Interviewing representatives of the agencies with experience in similar projects or in areas where the project is being carried out
- Learning firsthand about the general area by reading local newspapers, walking the streets, and getting to know a diverse range of individuals in and around the project area.

During this familiarization period, the evaluators refine their thinking about issues to be explored and methods to be used in the light of what they learn about the project setting.

2. Adapt Methods to the Project and Its Needs

An early decision is where to position evaluators to gain the confidence of project beneficiaries and learn from them about key issues of concern to management. For the projects discussed here, there was agreement among World Bank staff, local project personnel, and myself that on-site participant observation would be very useful in evaluating the slum upgrading and new housing. But for the artisan or home improvement credit components, conversational interviews including some specific questions made more sense. In general, when a project has several interrelated effects on one community (as in a slum improvement) and when the project is experimental (so that much is unknown about how the community may react), a participant observer who spends time living with project beneficiaries is likely to provide useful insights to managers. When the intended beneficiaries of a project are geographically dispersed and the project is narrowly focused (as in a credit program), however, conversational interviewing alone may be more appropriate.

Conversational interviews are also preferable when the presence of a participant observer living among beneficiaries would be obtrusive. In Bangkok one component of the urban project being evaluated was a slum relocation involving neighborhoods of no more than a hundred households. The evaluation was to gauge people's reactions to the removal and the cost to them of transport and loss of employment. Clearly, an outsider living in the midst of such a small number of relocating families would attract undue attention and perhaps distort the project by his very presence. Similarly, in Guasmo Norte (chapter 3), where community leaders had rejected the project for political reasons two years earlier, a resident participant observer would have attracted excessive attention. His ongoing involvement with the community as an emissary of project institutions would have appeared to challenge the authority of the neighborhood's political leaders.

The objective of participant-observer evaluation is to bring the people's perspective to the managers in time to alter the course of the program. Evaluation of a community upgrading project using on-site participant observation should require a period of residence of two to three months. Qualitative interviewing will require less time, depending on the size of the sample. Each interview should take roughly twenty to thirty minutes. To establish trust, the same person may be interviewed two or three times. The observation, participation, and open interview methods most commonly used in participant-observer evaluation are woven together, with quantitative procedures generally following an initial exploratory phase.

For example, when I first lived in the low-cost public housing area of Floresta in Guayaquil, I was not sure what issues to address, although general guidelines had been established. By the end of the first three months one issue stood out: there was no dialogue between the residents and representatives of the Housing Bank which was managing the project. World Bank and project officials agreed that this issue warranted further inquiry. Part of the reason for this lack of dialogue may have been the uncommunicative stance of the Housing Bank, a problem that was beyond the scope of my work; another part presumably lay with the beneficiaries among whom I was living. Upon my return for the second period of residence I resolved to know more about how the residents of this project related to each other and to their local leaders. Although I could learn something about these issues from participation in meetings and observation of my own pathway, I needed some systematic and quantitative assessment of what was taking place in other pathways. Hence an interview format was devised that, among other things, sought to elicit comments from the residents about the nature of their interaction with neighbors and their elected representative and their opinions about the value of this interaction. The resulting qualitative survey took my local assistants and me two weeks to complete. Findings expressed in descriptive and numerical terms were incorporated in the final report one month later (summarized in chapter 3).

Most basic to the participant-observer evaluation approach is keeping eyes and ears open and learning from listening. After a series of interviews in Guasmo Fertisa in Guayaquil about how much people were willing to pay for piped-in water, some women talking among themselves in my presence revealed an issue I hadn't thought to raise in the interview: the fear of assuming any significant financial obligation because of the widely fluctuating earnings characteristic of the urban poor.[4] This fear helped explain why many people in low-income urban settlements were willing to pay much more for water from trucks than for water piped to their houses. I learned this not by asking, but by listening. William Foote Whyte noted the same phenomenon in his classic, *Street Corner Society*: "As I sat and listened, I learned the answers to questions that I would not even have had the sense to ask if I had been getting my information solely on an interviewing basis."[5]

3. Blend Qualitative and Quantitative Information

Numbers deliver a message in ways that pure description often does not. Living with the people of 8 de Diciembre, I could see the neighborhood being transformed by home improvements. I came to understand from the people themselves that all this private construction stemmed partly from pride, partly from the desire for rental income. These motivations were best made concrete by numerical measures: (1) the percentage of 8 de Diciembre homes that had undergone improvement (67 percent) compared with the proportion in three similar communities during the same time (an average of 12 percent), all derived by simple counting; (2) the rise in the proportion of households containing renters over the three years of the project (from 30 to 80 percent of the total), obtained from adding up responses to survey interviews; and (3) the percentage of total household income for the residents of the upgrading area represented by rental income (an average of 30 percent), again derived from simple computation of responses to conversational interviews.

These quantities, together with the understanding gained from knowing how the people perceive and react to the project, provide a statement about the worth of this project. As Michael Scriven points out, "Good evaluation is the systematic, comprehensive, objective determination of merit or worth."[6] Worth is a matter of judgment and measurement, quality and quantity. Recent evaluation literature has recognized the advisability of combining qualitative and quantitative methods in evaluation research and of seeing each as complementary rather than antagonistic to the other.[7] This blend is still rare in international development work, however, where the preference has been for largely quantitative evaluation, despite considerable dissatisfaction with the results.[8]

4. Focus on Issues of Concern to Managers

Participant-observer evaluation explores significant issues on which decisionmakers want information, often from the perspective of the beneficiaries. The following questions are apt to be pertinent in many sectors:

How have project inputs been used and perceived by beneficiaries?
What is the beneficiaries' understanding of their role in the project?
How has the project changed the quality of life, at work and at home?
Why, according to the beneficiaries, have these changes occurred?
How do beneficiaries feel about interaction with project execution staff?
What suggestions do beneficiaries have for project improvement?

The issue and the manner of presenting it should evoke the maximum response possible on a range of related matters. The task of the interviewer is more to interpret the comments and behavior of the respondent than to pose questions. For participant-observer evaluation, good listeners make good interviewers.

5. Be Aware of Goals, Not Bound by Them

The focus in participant-observer evaluation is on what the project does in relation to what the people need. The goals of a project reveal what its designers intended it to do. Once a project is in operation, however, the actual effects it has on the population may be far different from those intended. The goals are useful as a point of reference but not as benchmarks against which progress should be measured.[9] There is a vast difference between the broad goals concerning institutional development and improvement in living conditions and the actual output, such as new houses, infrastructure, or increased crop yield. And what actually takes place in a beneficiary population during implementation of the project often has little to do with either goals or output.

Several findings in La Paz and Guayaquil would not have been made if the evaluations had focused exclusively on goal achievement. The entire subject of renters fell outside the normal purview of the La Paz project, since the beneficiaries had been expected to be homeowners. Neither the increase in rental housing nor the lack of access of many renters to project benefits were envisaged in project documents. But once reported, their importance was generally recognized by project staff, both in Bolivia and at the World Bank. Community organization—to mobilize communal efforts in public works projects in La Paz or to promote the project in Guasmo Norte—was not seen as a project goal (or as a means) in either place, but once highlighted by the evaluation its utility was appreciated by all concerned as being relevant to project success.

One question that all managers recognize as worthy of evaluation is, Are the people satisfied with a project? If so, why? If not, why not? Perhaps because the concept of satisfaction is considered to be simple it is rarely mentioned among project goals. Yet it is basic to evaluation. People attribute worth to that which gives them satisfaction. As George Santayana noted, "Satisfaction is the touchstone of value."[10] The generality and open-endedness of this question of satisfaction makes it an appropriate one for evaluation. It is also very other-directed. If an interviewer expresses interest in a person's satisfaction with a project, this concern for the individual's feelings and well-being allows him or her complete freedom in phrasing the response. Satisfaction may also be expressed by actions. In 8 de Diciembre indications of satisfaction were the decision of all homeowners to remain rather than profit from the sale of the dramatically appreciated land, and the high percentage of families making home improvements. These actions clearly demonstrated the worth of the project to the residents and its success.

Essentially, the driving force behind evaluation, and its rationale, is its utility in bringing about project improvements and thereby improving the living conditions of intended beneficiaries. Because of the importance of unforeseen and side effects over time, this utility is seriously reduced if the evaluation views a project's results primarily in relation to its previously set goals. Michael Quinn Patton makes this point in his useful book, *Practical Evaluation*: "The form of an evaluation should follow its function, not vice-versa, and evaluation has many functions, only some of which relate to goals."[11]

6. Place a Premium on Establishing Trust

The evaluator's physical proximity to the beneficiaries is crucial, as is his or her openness to them. The importance of gaining the trust of both the project implementors and the community in the early stages of the evaluation cannot be overstressed. The key is to be forthright about oneself and the nature of the evaluation from the outset. The confidence that is won by this open stance provides the basis for the interaction needed to view project activities from the perspective of the beneficiaries.

In recognizing the value of research that is based on empathy, trust, and experience participant observers take a lesson from anthropologists, who came to recognize that close observation and empathic participation were the keys to accurate understanding of those they studied. Anthropology emerged as a distinct discipline and declared itself a science when it rejected the distant "armchair" methods of earlier social researchers. Participative, in-depth research methods were adopted by anthropologists when they realized that they could not understand what they and others were seeing until they gained a certain competence in the cultural views of the people they studied. Participant-observer evaluation follows their lead for the same reason and because traditional evaluations often report facts that are not well understood and hence do not provide sufficient or correct basis for action.

To some degree, then, the participant-observer evaluator must become a member of the group he (or she) studies. To do this he needs to make some intellectual and emotional transference—that is, he needs to gain some understanding of what it means to think and feel as a member of that social group. The evaluator must develop rapport with the subjects of the evaluation. These people must come to see and accept the evaluator as a person (more or less like themselves) rather than as a professional. Out of this rapport, which borders on and may lead to friendship, comes the trust needed to understand the people's point of view. People opened up to me far more because of my relationship to them than because of what I was trying to do. As William Whyte noted, "I found that my acceptance in the district depended on the personal relationships I developed far more than upon any explanations I might give. . . . If I was all right, then my project was all right; if I was no good, then no amount of explanation could convince them that the book was a good idea."[12]

To establish trust one should be nonthreatening and open to others. The evaluator who lives in the project area or conducts qualitative interviews there may receive ready access to the community, and yet he provokes instant suspicion. On the one hand, the people are pleased, some even complimented, when a representative of the project elicits their opinions about it. A common reaction among people of both 8 de Diciembre and Floresta was appreciation for my presence: "This is a good thing you are doing," they would tell me. "If only the project [implementing unit] had sent someone to live with us for a while, as you are doing, this project would have been far better than it is." People like to talk with an interested listener about a project that is transforming their environment. The people's own interest in the subject of the interview, the betterment of their community, also gives them the incentive to address the interview topics seriously.[13]

On the other hand, an individual attached in some way to institutions that finance or execute the project may be seen as investigating the people. In the upgrading community in La Paz, weeks passed before some of my more skeptical neighbors were assured that I was not an auditor verifying that public works were built according to plans and regulations and that people were paying for them as they were contractually obligated to do. I was always aware of the importance of providing assurance that I was not living in the community to spy on the people there.

Establishing close rapport with a few key individuals in the community does much to establish credibility. These persons will serve as crucial reference points, generating new insights and confirming information gathered from other sources. In anthropology these persons are known as informants—a designation that focuses excessively on the utilitarian nature of the relationship. Both for credibility in the community and for the reliability of information received, however, the relationship should be based primarily on an affinity that is the precursor of friendship.[14]

The immense value of at least one very close relationship in the community being studied is seen in the close association between William Whyte and Doc in *Street Corner Society*, Elliot Liebow and Tally in *Tally's Corner*,[15] and Oscar Lewis and the Sánchez family in *The Children of Sánchez*.[16] Although none of these works is project-oriented, each is a very good example of the manner in which in-depth information and credibility in a community come from establishing close trust and friendship with one or a few individuals.

Establishing credibility is a constant preoccupation in operational evaluation. The observer's clothing, comportment, speech, and attitude must be acceptable and not provoke suspicion or create too much distance. Where there are social or political subgroupings, as there invariably are, the observer should not become overly identified with any one group so as not to obstruct information from the others. The role of a participant observer in the evaluation of a development project may be described as diplomatic, investigative journalism oriented to the design and management of poverty programs. This kind of work, while highly stimulating, is a real strain on the individual undertaking it. He or she is always on stage. A good participant observer must always be aware that he is being observed as well. How he conducts himself, at all times, will be interpreted by members of the community as a reflection of his character and trustworthiness. And the way others perceive the participant observer ultimately determines the quality of his work. This calls for constant vigilance—he must be disarming but keep his guard up at the same time.[17]

One illustration from fieldwork I did while living in a tenement slum in Rio de Janeiro shows what *not* to do to win credibility. I had just moved into a small room, one of twenty-four cubicles on two floors, each rented by a different household. Although I had been careful to leave behind any expensive clothes, I had brought a small portable typewriter to write my observations at the end of each day. The evening of the third day I returned to find that the typewriter had been stolen and recovered in damaged state by a neighbor. Other neighbors who gathered around remarked that they had heard me use the machine and I should be more careful in the future. Presumably, my neighbors knew I was not so poor as they. Nevertheless, that typewriter had cost as much as they earned in a month and required a degree of literacy and training few of them or of their children would ever have. I felt the possession of the typewriter called attention to tangible differences between my neighbors and myself that otherwise might more easily have been discounted. Whether I sensed this situation correctly or not, I have used pen and paper for notetaking ever since.

7. Serve as a Bridge between Management and Beneficiaries

Too often evaluation is conducted by a division of the implementing unit that is far removed from management. The evaluation seems to be done as an end unto itself; it answers questions posed by the evaluators but is of little importance to the decisionmakers. Findings of this kind of evaluation, not surprisingly, receive little attention from management. The participant-observer evaluation must involve project management from start to finish.[18] This involvement is essential:

- At the outset, to determine the topics to be addressed and to select evaluators
- During implementation of the evaluation, to review interim findings and participate in discussions to alter the course of the evaluation once it is under way
- At the conclusion of the evaluation, to review the final report of observations and findings. Ideally, this report is first made orally, after which changes are made to take the perspective of management into account.

The evaluation also must have credibility among the beneficiaries. The premise is that both management and beneficiaries agree on the broad goals of the development project (such as raising incomes, improving health, or providing housing). The distance between the two groups, however, is such that actual operations may fall short of realizing these goals. The participant-observer evaluation acts as a broker between project goals and reality, bringing each closer to the other through a forceful, accurate, and practical presentation of what actually occurs in the light of what should be occurring. Thus, despite the service nature of participant-observer evaluation, it must have autonomy to function well.

The participant-observer evaluator must walk a fine line so as not to be unduly influenced by either project management or beneficiaries. This neutral role is often best played by outside consultants who, though paid or approved by management, are more likely to operate as independent parties and to be viewed as such. Independent judgment is ultimately in the best interests of sound evaluation, which should focus on whether conditions are or are not being improved rather than on the individuals who are managing or benefiting from the improvements. Although the participant-observer evaluator must know management, project, and beneficiaries well, his allegiance is to none of the three, but rather to what the project is meant to be.

The experience in the two urban projects in Bolivia and Ecuador and in the second generation of participant-observer evaluations in Bolivia, Brazil, and Thailand has demonstrated that evaluation is most useful when geared to the major concerns of project management. These concerns often revolve around the behavior of the people—the actual or intended beneficiaries—which is simply not understood from where the manager sits. Management may be either the sponsors or the implementors of the project, or both.

The question underlying a number of evaluations was why the intended beneficiaries failed to participate as expected. This was the particular concern of the World Bank regarding the rejected upgrading project in Guasmo Norte; the piso-techo housing in Guayaquil and in Thailand, which was not being inhabited as quickly as expected; and the fishing cooperatives in Brazil, which attracted only one-fifth of the fishermen whom they were intended to serve. Around these concerns small interview guides were formed.

In Guasmo Norte, for example, the interviewers were instructed to frame their conversations as follows:

> Do you remember a project of the municipality which was to have brought water and landfill to Guasmo Norte about two or three years ago?

Did you live in Guasmo Norte in early 1980?

(For those who did) What happened? Why didn't the project take place?

These simple lead-in questions, together with even less structured interviews with local leaders, led to the findings of the largely political reasons why the project was not accepted in this low-income area of Guayaquil (see chapter 3).

Part of the initial phase of participant-observer evaluation, getting to know the setting, should be devoted to establishing rapport between evaluators and project management. Given the holistic nature of participant-observer evaluation and the intangible, subjective matters it must interpret, management's opinion of the competence and honesty of the evaluators goes a long way in determining how much influence the evaluation findings will have. Periodic discussions of the findings between evaluators and management provide ongoing feedback, allow managers to change the nature and focus of the evaluation as it proceeds, and deepen the relationship of trust and understanding between evaluators and managers.

8. Strive for Reliability Rather than Precision

The manager needs as much information as is required to make a decision. The quantity of information and the precision with which it is recorded and presented are, however, far less important than the quality and reliability of the findings. Interviews should be recorded (in writing) away from the respondent so as to preserve the more natural setting and the possibility of observing the respondent's expression and behavior, which could easily be missed in the process of notetaking. The loss of accuracy in the recording is more than made up for by the enhanced quality and hence reliability of the interview.[19] In addition, as Robert Chambers points out in his highly practical essay on information gathering for rural projects, it is important to know what is not worth knowing and to avoid the frequent mistake of gathering excessive information. Similarly, it is more important to identify orders of magnitude and trends than aim for a "degree of accuracy which is unnecessary."[20]

The interpretation of survey data is crucial. For example, initial surveys showed a dramatic difference between 8 de Diciembre and San Antonio in the average length of time people had lived in La Paz. This information was only of passing interest until a local research assistant surmised that it was a factor in the low value San Antonio's recent urban immigrants placed on water and sewerage systems, compared with the more urbanized residents of 8 de Diciembre. To cite another example, although the initial survey in 8 de Diciembre found that 71 percent of households had "participated in community improvement work," subsequent discussions revealed that this had normally consisted of little more than the filling-in of ditches in front of a household's plot. The precise percentage gave the impression of accuracy but was shown by further contextual understanding to be misleading. Especially when the phenomena observed are complex and subject to widely varying interpretation, as in the case of community participation, it is far better to give a reliable if general picture of what actually takes place than to present precise numerical measures out of context.

The best way to ensure reliability is to cross-check findings, that is, to compare them with information collected in other ways. Evaluation specialists call this "triangulation." Both qualitative and quantitative techniques are used, and information can be triangulated in at least four different ways: using various sources of information, using different researchers, approaching the issue from the perspective of different theories, and studying a particular problem with different methodologies.[21]

In La Paz and Guayaquil I applied the concept of triangulation by:

- Verifying insights gained from participant observation with quantitative, more generalized data gathered from structured interviews
- Utilizing at least three interviewers on any survey
- Taking into account the perspectives both of executing agency officials and of various community members—selected so as to represent main subgroups of class, income, geographical location, and political leaning—in arriving at a conclusion
- Comparing findings in various specific locales.

The dual challenge the participant-observer evaluator faces when gathering information is: does it matter? and is it true? If the answers to both questions are positive, the evaluation is useful to project management. The incorporation of management into the design and monitoring of the evaluation helps ensure its relevance. With regard to the second question, on reliability, participant-observer evaluation seldom needs to go beyond simple statistical rules of sampling and the derivation of mean, median, and mode.[22]

The project manager or officer, in the field or in a central bureaucracy, makes decisions based on many assumptions or hunches. The project is necessarily carried out in a context that is constantly changing and imperfectly understood. Participant-observer evaluation provides the development professional with information that may be used to bring the operating assumptions closer to the project reality than they would be otherwise. The managers are not looking for statistical proof to help them make good decisions. Indeed, they realize that many factors about which they need knowledge do not lend themselves to scientific tests of validity. Rather, project managers seek reasonable explanations of behavioral and natural phenomena that, together with their own working hypotheses, may guide their decisions.

The entire evaluation process in Guasmo Norte, from initial discussions to survey to concluding interviews with local and government officials, took less than one month. The establishment of confidence with the Floresta residents who had relatives in Guasmo took another two months. In three months' time, conclusions were reached about a project that had been stymied for almost three years. Despite the brevity of the actual fieldwork and the rudimentary nature of the statistical methods employed, these findings were judged valid by both local and World Bank officials, who made radical changes in the nature of the project as a result.

All the other main findings reported in this book were made in the same hybrid manner, with a blend of simple techniques focused on issues of importance to the project's success. The reaction of managers was generally not to call for more scientific proof but rather to express confidence in the validity of the findings as presented. More significantly, on the basis of the findings they took actions and formed policies to remedy the problems on which the evaluation had focused.

« »

Participant-observer evaluation of development projects is an attempt to blend qualitative and quantitative methods of analyses so as to be useful to decisionmakers and ultimately beneficial to the poor majorities for whom development assistance is carried out. Implicit in this approach is an attempt to move beyond conceptual and methodological barriers created by evaluation typologies (formative or summative, process or impact)[23] and to transcend dichotomies (we-they, subject-object, anthropologist-economist, professional-beneficiary). Participant-observer evaluation methods must closely follow those of ethnography, the field of social anthropology that has been referred to as "neither 'subjective' nor 'objective'" but "interpretive, mediating two worlds through a third." Michael Agar describes ethnography as "unique among the social sciences" in that "it is committed to making sense out of the way informants naturally talk and act when they are doing ordinary activities rather than activities imposed by a researcher."[24]

This basic understanding of people on their own terms and as they relate to planned intervention is the core of participant-observer evaluation. The methods described here help bring about the necessary rapport between observer and beneficiary to obtain reliable interpretations of behavior, and they provide insights that contribute to management and policy decisions relating to these beneficiaries. This process has been called "grounded theory" or "the building of generalizations out of a particular body of data."[25] This, of course, is what managers must do every day; as they observe events, they make working hypotheses, which become the bases for decisions. Participant observation has also been seen as a process of analytic induction which "formalizes and systematizes the method of the working hypothesis."[26]

Insofar as participant-observer evaluation brings to light the findings of empirical study in relation to decisionmakers' needs, it has much in common with "illustrative evaluation."[27] By drawing upon particular observations to form generalizations, which in turn lead to working hypotheses, participant-observer evaluation has the advantage of being able to adapt to changing circumstances over time; that is, the nature of the inquiry can change in accordance with the evolving needs of decisionmakers.[28] Because development projects are carried out in rapidly changing environments, they need to be evaluated with enough flexibility to take account of this changing situation. Experimental designs that measure project-induced change according to pre-established indices and against pre-established hypotheses—and even questionnaires with their predetermined wording, ordering, and categories—are not adaptive to change. Participant observation, with its inherent openness to the context being observed, "is especially useful in one particular research context—the study of the dynamics of a social organization or situation."[29]

The two basic methods—conversational interviewing and participant observation, including residence with beneficiaries—are intended to increase the reliability and relevance of evaluation and hence its utility to decisionmakers in the development field. The basic problem with questionnaires is the artificiality of the interview setting. People are simply not apt to disclose important information about themselves to someone they do not know, regardless of the stated purpose of obtaining the information. "Most sensible people do not believe what a stranger tells them."[30] People are especially reluctant to talk openly on controversial matters if they feel the information might be used against them or if they are in any way embarrassed about public disclosure of the information. Poor people in developing countries (project beneficiaries) are, from experience, distrustful of anyone in authority or anyone who appears to be working for those in authority. And they are not comfortable about disclosing certain aspects of their lives to middle-class interviewers standing at their door with pencil and paper in hand. The poor are least ready to be open about their health and sanitation practices, attitudes and behavior regarding birth control, and, as is well known, income—topics that are particularly important to developmental decisionmakers.[31]

Conversational interviewing, with its more natural setting, and, where possible, on-site residence among project beneficiaries have been shown in the preceding chapters to provide project managers with useful, timely, and low-cost information with which to make project improvements. Participant-observer evaluation also includes reviews of second-hand sources of information, such as the minutes of meetings or correspondence, direct observation, and even minimal socioeconomic questionnaire surveys. It consciously blends qualitative and quantitative methods of analysis. Although this approach appears to be gaining favor in developing countries,[32] it is still far from being the dominant mode of evaluating international development programs.[33] But participant-observer evaluation has been shown to work. It is recommended whenever people want to learn from others for their mutual interest.

« **8** »

Conclusion

Participant-observer evaluation fills a void in international development work. In the past, managers who attempted to understand the social environment affected by a development project have generally relied on cursory visits by staff, before-after evaluations with an experimental design, or statistical measurements of project output. These procedures have not sufficiently revealed the reality of a project. Project staff often fail to gain the needed understanding of beneficiary groups because their own identification with the project colors their vision and impedes free communication. Traditional impact evaluations typically take too long for results to be useful to managers. These evaluations have used large, costly sample surveys and complex statistical work. Although rigorous, they have generally failed to provide conclusive evidence that whatever impact was detected was due to the project's interventions rather than to other changes in the environment extraneous to the project.

Most important, these evaluations fail to provide information about how a particular project activity is perceived by the beneficiaries—a basic concern of managers seeking to make the project more effective. The primary strength of participant-observer evaluation is in the assessment of people's perceptions in relation to a planned or ongoing project.

The strict dichotomy made in evaluation literature between "process" and "impact" evaluations is often overdrawn. Development projects affect people's lives over time; they are generally experimental in nature, operating in social and economic environments that are constantly changing, irrespective of the project intervention. Often the first few years of a project are spent on getting inputs, such as houses, infrastructure, and irrigation systems, in place and in use. Projects that intervene in people's lives in major ways are unlikely to have measurable impacts, such as changed health or income, that can readily be ascribed to the projects themselves within the first five to ten years of operation. Inasmuch as development sets in motion or furthers processes whereby people become increasingly able to improve their own living conditions, the elucidation of trends and directions of change is more germane than the before-after or ex post measurement of impact.

This is not to say that other approaches to evaluation do not have legitimacy. There are times, especially in the case of large-scale programs affecting many people, when it will be necessary to measure the impact and questionnaires will be called for. Certain project components—those providing particular, quantitative results—will lend themselves to cost-benefit analysis. At strategic junctures in a project's history the need may be for a rapid, cursory examination of one feature of the project that entails simple counting.

Generally, however, development managers need something midway between spurious, short-cut head counting and extensive, comprehensive field studies. What is wanted is an effective manner to bring people into the planning and implementation of programs that affect their lives. The methods of limited participant observation and conversational interviewing of representative samples of a given population—these open, listening modes of inquiry referred to in this book as participant-observer evaluation—are attempts to reach this middle way.

Participant-observer evaluation constructs a series of in-depth interpretations of a real situation being affected by a project so that managers and policymakers may understand the nature of change produced in time to decide on continued support for such change. In the upgrading project in La Paz, measurements were made of home improvements, number of renters in the area, and general satisfaction with the project at several points in time. All three factors were found to have increased to a greater degree than expected by outside observers. Self-help communal works of street paving and the construction of the community center, however, did not take place as expected. I sensed a pride of place, which led to the positive changes, but I also noted a lack of effective local leadership and organization needed to carry out the communal activities. By the time of my third visit, however, a consumer cooperative was operating and other activities were being planned. This ongoing, intermittent participant observation indicated that the upgrading stimulated self-help at an individual or household level before doing so at a community level. With this lesson in mind, project management made changes in other project areas of La Paz and actively organized neighborhoods to carry out communal development activities.

Participant-observer evaluation as described in this book is a simple way to relate the concerns of project beneficiaries to the concerns of project managers. The participant-observer evaluator acts as a broker; he or she attends to the effectiveness of the project in view of its goals in a particular context rather than to either beneficiaries or managers as distinct interest groups. The underlying assumption of participant-observer evaluation is that managers do not normally have an adequate understanding of the world they are trying to change. This understanding is found primarily among the people who inhabit that world. To gain this understanding managers need to seek assistance from third parties who can relate the operational needs of the project to the social environment being affected. These third parties learn mostly from the people—by asking their opinions, listening to them talk about the project, and sharing the people's own project experiences.

Participant-observer evaluation uses both qualitative and quantitative techniques, as needed, to convey to the decisionmaker an accurate picture of the real situation. Participant-observer evaluation recognizes the need to reach out to the people in such a way that they may speak freely about their own concerns. Openness is the stance. Closeness to the people is the position. The methods of participant observation and conversational interviewing are tools to derive understanding. Often the most useful insights come more from the observer's proximity to the people, his acceptance by them and openness to them, than from the application of the tools themselves. The numbers come after the listening, not before. For participant-observer evaluation, numbers are not abstractions; they emerge from and help to illustrate what a project means to the people for whom it is intended.

The partial reliance of this approach on qualitative methods opens it to charges of subjectivity and distortion because of the presumed biases of the individual conducting the evaluation. Although bias may also adversely color more purely quantitative procedures (where it is more likely to be concealed under a patina of authoritative numbers), it is a legitimate issue which needs to be addressed. Biases may affect the selection of respondents and of topics for inquiry as well as the interpretation of people's words or behavior in a project setting. Pure objectivity is an unobtainable and unreal goal. A degree of bias is inherent in all commentary on human affairs. Bias can, however, be diminished in participant-observer evaluation by the selection of sound, experienced observers, the use of triangulation (discussed in chapter 7), and the participation of project management at all key points in the design and execution of the investigation.

The information elicited by this directed listening has led to project improvements wherever participant-observer evaluation has been conducted. The La Paz upgrading project not only increased its community organization activities as a result of findings from the evaluation but also changed contracts with homeowners to make infrastructure connections mandatory for renters, thereby improving sanitation for both renters and owners. Information from the misconceived upgrading effort in Guasmo Norte was instrumental in changing the Guayaquil project to provide more institutional support to the municipality. Also in Guayaquil, the Ecuadorian Housing Bank increased its outreach into slum areas to promote the project among low-income families and increase collection rates. Upon receiving feedback on the causes of low occupancy rates in the partially completed piso-techo houses, the Housing Bank increased its credit lines (and income requirements) for a second, larger group of buyers of core units. Similar findings on this same phenomenon in Thailand have led the National Housing Authority to phase out partially completed units in subsequent housing projects in favor of immediately habitable houses. Participant-observer evaluation findings in Brazil led to decisions to mount major promotional campaigns among fishing cooperatives in Natal and to construct improved latrines in Recife on the basis of people's expressed willingness to pay for them.

Participant-observer evaluation is widely applicable because it may be conducted by host-country nationals. Local persons carried out this kind of evaluation in urban projects in Brazil and Thailand and rural projects in Bolivia. Men and women trained in a variety of disciplines, such as agronomy, anthropology, architecture, economics, sociology, social work, and urban planning, evaluated projects by using the methods of participant observation and conversational interviewing to interpret the concerns and reactions of low-income beneficiaries to project management.

Many of the findings of the participant-observer evaluations involved intangibles that would most likely have been ignored by a measurement-oriented quantitative approach. Examples include the difference between community leaders and the rank and file of the residents (Guayaquil and Recife); the burden of monthly payments on the underemployed (Guayaquil); the friction that arises when a project site is adjacent to an unserviced community (Guayaquil and La Paz); and the crucial role of fish merchants in dissuading fishermen from joining fishing cooperatives (Natal).

Other findings came from the traditional application of questionnaires, yet their reliability and contextual significance were enhanced by the use of more qualitative methods to supplement the quantitative analysis. Rapid, door-to-door surveys may produce an estimate of renters in an area, but because renters are a somewhat hidden subgroup, their real significance and the degree to which they receive infrastructure and add to homeowners' income may best be understood by using qualitative methods. In other cases purely quantitative techniques may obtain correct data (the number of homes being improved in an area receiving infrastructure), yet the factors which lead to the phenomenon (pride in one's own house and the status associated with improved neighborhoods) come to light only from knowing the people as well as the numbers.

Finally, participant-observer evaluation saves money. The evaluation itself has low costs for personnel and data processing. Even more significant are the savings realized in program operations when practical, timely feedback from beneficiaries helps expedite project execution, reduces the time necessary for staff supervision, and improves repayment rates and cost recovery. The seven evaluations done by host-country personnel in Bolivia, Brazil, and Thailand cost an average of $15,000 each, while the projects evaluated averaged $9 million in loan amounts. Almost 50 percent of the evaluations' cost in these first efforts was for guidance by World Bank personnel—a cost that will diminish appreciably over time as local institutions gain the expertise to conduct this kind of work on their own. These small costs were considered by management to be far outweighed by the benefits from the use of operational evaluation.

It should come as no surprise that the most successful project components observed were those most closely attuned to the people they were trying to help. The upgrading project in La Paz did best when it built on community leaders' pre-existing desires for improvements *and* their recognition of payment obligation. This project underwent constant improvements as it received useful feedback from the evaluation and from increasingly sensitive interaction with the leaders and ordinary citizens of the community. The private bank in Guayaquil had a dedicated group of urban extension workers whose job was to know the particular needs and capabilities of each artisan borrower. This credit program and that of the Housing Bank for home improvements in the same city were successful in providing benefits to low-income people in a potentially cost-recoverable fashion because they also built on pre-existing values, needs, and wants in workplaces and homes.

The relationship between the success of an endeavor and its closeness to people has been well demonstrated in the private sector. Thomas J. Peters and Robert H. Waterman point out in their recent review of America's best companies, *In Search of Excellence,* that the companies that do the best business are the most outwardly oriented, particularly in relation to their consumers: "The excellent company values almost always stress being close to the customer or are otherwise externally focused. Intense customer focus leads the prototypical excellent company to be unusually sensitive to the environment . . . The excellent companies are not only better on service, quality, reliability, and finding a niche. They are also better listeners."[1]

Managing a successful business and running a good development program have much in common. Both business and development should be concerned with improving people's lives in one way or another. The successful companies—and successful development projects—recognize that people generally know best what is best for them. The best technology serves people's needs; it does not create them.

« »

In one sense listening to the people transcends what is usually meant by the term evaluation. It is based on the commonsensical notion that before trying to develop a group of people it is necessary to understand them. The knowledge of people that is needed cannot be transmitted by statistics alone.

Inasmuch as development must become self-sustaining to be meaningful and people are the prime generators of their own development, development requires an appreciation of what leads people to improve their own lives. Values, which underlie attitudes and opinion and which may be prime motivators, are learned by closely observing people and sharing their experience over protracted periods of time. Perceptions also often determine behavior and, like values, they are learned by watching how people act and listening to what they say. Witnessing and listening require an unobtrusive, empathetic, and trusted observer, in unhurried contact with people.

In the field of international development as it is currently practiced, numbers and theories abound; so do the manipulators and practitioners for whom these are the tools of trade. Sorely missing, however, is the synthesis of thought and action revealed in the experience of beneficiaries. Learning from the experience of others—through sharing, listening, and observing, as was done for the projects reviewed in this book—has been shown to provide important lessons for guiding ongoing change. People are best able to tell their story in action and words where they work and live. To learn what they have to teach us about development, we must learn to observe carefully and listen to the people.

Appendixes

A. Steps in Conducting Participant-Observer Evaluation

1. *Become familiar with the background of the project.* What are the project's objectives? Why and how was the site or the target population chosen? How did the executing agency and beneficiary population come together? Sources for this information are documents and interviews with key representatives of funding and executing agencies and with beneficiary leaders at the time of the project's initiation.

2. *Learn the general characteristics of the population group benefiting from the project.* Determine the history of the area and of the people—their places of origin, reasons for coming to the area or project site, and length of residence. In obtaining a socioeconomic profile of population (age, sex, education, employment, income, health), be sure to sample for major internal divisions determined by such factors as location, status, and political affiliation.

3. *Choose a place of residence with care.* Live in a fairly central location; in an area that is being upgraded rent a place somewhat better than average, one that offers the basic comforts and a separate entry. For a single person it is best to live in association with a family, yet clearly independent of it, so as to blend more easily into and become a part of the community.

4. *Get to know the leading actors in the project well.* The important contacts will be with the beneficiaries in general, their formal and informal leaders, and the main administrators of the implementing agency. Attempt to keep relations with each of these groups somewhat discrete. The manner of

relating should be adapted to each—more professional with project administrators, less so with community leaders, and more informal with beneficiaries. Although everyone will know the reason for the observer's stay in the neighborhood, the official nature of that stay should be most apparent to the project personnel, with whom a certain degree of personal distance must be maintained to avoid bias, real or alleged, intentional or unconscious. The leaders will also be aware of the motive for the observer's presence, especially at the outset but less so over time. In some cases it may help credibility to have a letter signed by a government authority—not the executing agency but a more distant, neutral body. The people, however, should view the participant observer primarily as a neighbor and, to varying degrees, as a friend. At this level the relationship is far more personal than professional, although the people should be duly informed of why the observer is living among them.

Cultivate a few close contacts in diverse segments of the population representing various income groups, political factions, or other significant entities (such as youths, female heads of households, owners, and renters). Never be overly identified with any one group, but remain open and accessible to all: diplomacy at the neighborhood level.

Attempt to participate in community organizations and activities but without becoming overly committed. The observer's goal should be to demonstrate his involvement and have his efforts and interest appreciated, but to retain his independence.

5. *Inject issues of concern into discussions with residents after winning their confidence.* These issues will have been identified with funding and executing institutions before the observer's entry into the community and will be refined by the participant observer in conjunction with the executing agency while at the project site. These issues should be introduced into conversation, or spontaneous discussion of them encouraged, and the talk should be guided to focus on the project—all in as unobtrusive a manner as possible. The aim is always to serve as catalyst and to provoke the most honest response possible.

For instance, one issue that affected the diffusion of project benefits and even the viability of the upgrading projects themselves was the nature of community leadership in 8 de Diciembre and Guasmo. Although a sensitive topic, it had to be addressed to find out why certain project activities did or did not take place and why some people benefited but not others. Direct references to this issue at the outset of our stay, before we had gained the people's confidence, would surely have produced distorted responses.

Do not neglect the power of observation: Who actually participates in community improvement work? How are houses being improved? What is the quality of work performed by the executing agency? Photography will help illustrate observations.

6. *Elaborate one or more simple survey guides to help substantiate or determine what appear to be key findings.* This should be done in consultation with the implementing agency after becoming thoroughly familiar with the community and the way it has been affected by the project. Sample sizes should be barely representative, large enough to be taken seriously, not so large as to attract undue attention in the community. The data should be simple enough to process manually and in little time (not more than a week).

7. *Prepare a report.* The final report should include a description of the actual situation, key findings, conclusions, and recommendations. Before writing it, discussions should be held with community leaders and informants to verify the thrust of the report and with the implementation agency to understand issues from its perspective. If the report is to go to the funding agency, it should be shared first with the executing agency, not only as a matter of courtesy and ethics, but also to help win the agency's cooperation. Disagreements of the project implementors, if any, should be reflected in the report sent to sponsors.

B. Notes

Chapter 1

1. For a fuller description of World Bank urban projects, see World Bank, *Learning by Doing: World Bank Lending for Urban Development, 1972–82* (Washington, D.C., 1983).

Chapter 2

1. Dollar amounts are U.S. dollars throughout the book.

2. Spanish acronyms for the Honorable Alcaldia Municipal (HAM) and the Banco Internacional de Reconstrucción y Desarrollo (BIRF), the Spanish name of the World Bank, which is known formally as the International Bank for Reconstruction and Development.

3. Yolanda Barriga and Luisa Fernanda Rada lived in two areas in La Paz being upgraded, San Antonio and 16 de Julio, respectively; in Guayaquil, Hilda Sánchez de Gaviria lived in Floresta.

4. Fernando Calderón G. and Gonzalo Flores C., "Urbanización y Desarrollo: Necesidades Básicas en Areas Periféricas," UNICEF Serie Documentos no. 2 (La Paz, 1981), p. 15.

5. Centro Pastoral-Arquidiócesis de La Paz, "La Opción por los Pobres: Algunos Datos Socio-Económicos de la Realidad Boliviana" (La Paz, September 1979), p. 20.

6. Xavier Albo, Tomás Greaves, and Godofredo Sandoval, *Chukiyaqu, La Cara Aymara de La Paz: I. El Paso a la Ciudad,* CIPCA no. 20 (La Paz, 1981), p. 43.

7. Giovanni C. Mirabella, Gloria Ardaya, and others, "Factores Psicosociales de la Migración Rural Urbana" (La Paz: Centro de Estudios de la Realidad Económica y Social [CERES], October 1980), p. 69.

8. During the same period the dollar rose in value 1,000 percent against the Bolivian peso. Inasmuch as low-income persons bought few imported goods, this declining rate of exchange of the Bolivian peso affected them far less than it did more affluent members of the society or businesses dependent on imports (interview with Mahmood Ayub, resident representative of the World Bank for Bolivia, La Paz, February 28, 1983).

9. Honorable Alcaldia Municipal (HAM) de La Paz, *Plan de Desarrollo Urbano-Ciudad de La Paz, vol.3, Esquema Urbano* (La Paz, 1978), p. 24; Calderón and Flores, "Urbanización y Desarrollo," p. 30.

10. Centro Pastoral, "La Opción por los Pobres," p. 23.

11. Calderón and Flores, "Urbanización y Desarrollo," p. 32.

12. Alberto Rivera, "Pachamama Expensive: El Contexto Territorial Urbano y la Diferenciación Social en la Ciudad de La Paz, 1971–1976" (La Paz: CERES, October 1981), p. 79; and Calderón and Flores, "Urbanización y Desarrollo," p. 32–33.

13. Comparable figures for all peripheral areas are 38 and 57 percent, respectively, with 5 percent not speaking Spanish at all (Calderón and Flores, "Urbanización y Desarrollo," pp. 23–24.

14. The municipality's development plan gave ninety square meters as the average space per inhabitant of La Paz in 1976 (HAM, *Plan de Desarrollo,* p. 33).

15. Gaitán Villavicencio and Diego Carrión, "Acciones de los Sectores Populares Frente al Problema de la Tierra Urbana y Reacciones de las Fuerzas Socio-Políticas Afectadas: El Caso de Quito y Guayaquil," Documento HABQUI, no. 30, p. 5, and Alicia Ponce and Hernán Valencia, "Configuración del Espacio Regional Ecuatoriano y Desarrollo Urbano de Quito y Guayaquil," Documento HABQUI, no. 19, p. 9; both papers were prepared for the third seminar on African–Latin American Precarious Human Settlements, Quito, October 1981.

16. Caroline O. N. Moser, "A Home of One's Own: Squatter Housing Strategies in Guayaquil, Ecuador," in Alan Gilbert and others, eds., *Urbanization in Contemporary Latin America: Critical Approaches to the Analysis of Urban Issues* (New York: Wiley, 1982), pp. 165–66.

17. Richard James Thomas Moore, "Assimilation and Political Participation among the Urban Poor in Guayaquil, Ecuador," Ph.D. dissertation, University of Texas, December 1977, pp. 119–20; Fernando Rosero, Martha Moscoso, and Arturo Maldonado, "Investigación Socio-Económica de los Barrios Suburbanos de Guayaquil" (Quito: Ministerio de Bienestar Social y Promoción Popular, July 1981), pp. 18–30, 132, 237, and 719.

18. Carlos Luzuriaga, "Issues of Human Settlement in Ecuador" (Quito: U.S. Agency for International Development, November 1980), p. 36.

19. Ibid., p. 31.

20. Ponce and Valencia, "Configuración del Espacio Regional Ecuatoriano," p. 11.

21. Unidad Ejecutora Municipal Departamento Social, "Síntesis del Primer Proyecto de Desarrollo Urbano de Guayaquil" (Guayaquil, February 1982; processed), p. 2.

22. *El Universo*, June 27, 1983, p. 2.

23. Roldos died tragically in an airplane crash on May 24, 1981, at the age of forty. The Plan Roldos was "the only formal-sector housing project ever built for the poor in Guayaquil" (Jorge Salomón, "El Problema de la Vivienda en Guayaquil: Implicaciones y Soluciones" [Guayaquil, August 25, 1982], pp. 3–4).

24. As of February 1982, of 104 families that had lived in Floresta no more than four months, 47 percent had already increased the size of their house (usually by half) and another 51 percent planned to do so later; for Floresta and Los Sauces, 98 percent fell into both categories. Marcos Arteaga, "Investigación de los Adjudicatarios del Plan Roldos de Vivienda Popular Respecto a los Niveles Social, Económico y Espacial en Su Situación Actual: Relación Proyección Vivencial en Cuanto a la Unidad de Vivienda Adquirida" (Guayaquil, March 1982; processed), p. 70. My own surveys taken in November 1982 and July 1983 corroborated this data.

25. Figures for Guayaquil extrapolated from household surveys done by the Instituto Nacional de Estadística (1975), adjusted for changes in the value of the currency and earnings in the intervening time, and from interviews with Gaitán Villavicencio, economist, Guayaquil, October 1982.

Chapter 3

1. Ponce and Valencia, "Configuración del Espacio Regional Ecuatoriano," p. 23; Jorge Salomón, "Estudio Socio-Económico de Guasmo Norte" (Municipality of Guayaquil, October 1981), pp. 14–18, 24.

2. Rosero, Moscoso, and Maldonado, "Investigación Socio-Económica de los Barrios Suburbanos de Guayaquil, " p. 298.

3. Roldos's deep concern for the housing needs of Guayaquil's poor was mentioned by World Bank staff and by John Klein, former general director, Banco Ecuatoriano de la Vivienda, a personal friend of the late president, in an interview November 19, 1982.

4. Interview with Jaime Vera, director, Municipal Executive Unit, October 25, 1982. During this interview I was shown a flipchart used in the meeting, which contained the words *agua domiciliar,* household water connections.

5. The sample was deliberately kept small to avoid raising expectations in the area, inasmuch as the decision had already been made not to upgrade the community.

6. A survey of the suburbios and Mapasingue stated that 59 percent of the sample cited drinking water as the single most important need (Moore, "Assimilation and Political Participation," p. 275); Jorge Salomón, "Descripción de las Reuniones de la Comunidad en Guasmo Norte" (Guayaquil: Municipal Executing Unit, February 1980), p. 1.

7. There is a difference of opinion on the attendance at the meetings in January

and February 1980. The written history of this episode states each meeting was attended by from 150 to 200 persons. If every attendee represented a separate household, more than 80 percent of the population of 8,800 of the time would have been covered (Salomón, "Descripción de las Reuniones," p. 1). However, various residents and an official of the municipality present at those meetings stated that attendance was low.

8. The monthly payment of 550 sucres was 14 percent of the average monthly family income of 3,946 sucres found in a survey conducted by the executing unit in mid-1978, a year and a half before the unit's meetings with the community. With intervening increases in salary this could have dropped to 12 percent, about twice the proportion of family income then spent for water from trucks (250 sucres).

9. Salomón, "Descripción de las Reuniones," pp. 9–11.

10. For a lucid discussion of politics and the low-income barrios of Guayaquil, see Gaitán Villavicencio, "Democracia, Populismo y Lucha: Reindicativas Urbanas: El Caso de Guayaquil (La Lucha por la Tierra y la Vivienda, 1978–1979)," in *Explotación y Miseria Urbana: La Lucha por la Tierra y la Vivienda en Guayaquil* (Guayaquil: Instituto de Investigaciones Económicas y Políticas, Universidad de Guayaquil, November 1980), pp. 305–15.

11. The fifty-six families (39 percent of the sample) who were willing to pay the stipulated 550 sucres a month earned an average of 8,257 sucres ($142) a month—more than one and a half (152 percent) times the average family earnings of 5,433 sucres ($94) of the majority (61 percent, or eighty-nine families) of the sample, who felt this payment to be excessive. (All figures are at the exchange rate of 58 sucres to the U.S. dollar.)

12. The survey did not include electricity payments, which are made monthly by most persons in Guasmo, but a survey conducted there in 1981 found electricity to be 1.2 percent of family expenditures, or about 80 sucres ($1.40) a month. (Rosero, Moscoso, and Maldonado, "Investigación Socio-Económica de los Barrios Suburbanos de Guayaquil," pp. 209–303).

13. "Water in Guayaquil costs two sucres a cubic meter for the rich while the price for the *suburbios* is 16 sucres a cubic meter" (*Diario El Expreso*, March 14, 1976). A World Bank report states that water from trucks costs twenty-five times that from pipes.

14. These nine families were later told that if they continued to refuse to participate in the project they would not be allowed by the municipality to sell their property at market value, not having contributed to the improvements which significantly raised property values (discussion with Jaime Medrano, director, HAM-BIRF, May 19, 1982).

15. According to HAM-BIRF, as a result of devaluation the monthly payments were so small ($2.50) that people simply neglected to pay on time, preferring to make lump payments every six months or so. I find this to be only a partial explanation of the high rates of arrears.

16. *Learning by Doing: World Bank Lending for Urban Development, 1972–82* (Washington, D.C.: World Bank, 1983), p. 31.

17. For many examples, see Thomas J. Peters and Robert H. Waterman, *In Search of Excellence: Lessons from America's Best-Run Companies* (New York: Harper and Row, 1982).

Chapter 4

1. Home improvement loans were a component of this project, but the amount (15,000 pesos) was devalued over my own two stays from $600 to less than $40. These funds were used mostly to rebuild walls torn down to make way for widening roads.

2. In less than two years local inflation climbed over 400 percent, most of the twenty major industries in La Paz closed down for lack of needed replacement parts and machinery (the peso was devalued against the dollar by over 1,200 percent in the parallel market during this period, and foreign exchange was almost nonexistent in Bolivia by early 1983), unemployment and underemployment climbed to an estimated record 40 percent of the active labor force, and few weeks passed without a strike as the main labor sectors—such as transport, education, commerce, and banking—agitated for a share of the rapidly dwindling economic pie.

3. Average family monthly income in March 1982 for 8 de Diciembre was about 5,000 pesos. With an estimated average increase of 150 percent in the intervening thirteen months, that amount would have been a little over 12,000 pesos ($61) by April 1983—a very small amount of money for a family averaging 5.7 persons.

4. This was a problem for many renters; see chapter 5.

5. The samples were approximately 10 percent of the total number of artisan borrowers benefiting from the World Bank projects in Guayaquil and La Paz at the time of this study (mid- to late 1982). These totals were 850 and 268, respectively.

6. This analysis is corroborated by experience and research findings in artisan credit programs in many developing countries, including Brazil, Burkina Faso, the Dominican Republic, and Panama (interviews with Shari Berenbach, program manager, Partnership for Productivity, and Bruce Tippett, founder of UNO in Northeast Brazil, July 23 and 19, 1984, respectively).

7. Interviews with Alexis de Aguilar, chief, Artisan Credit Program, August 24, 1982, and Rafael Cuesta, manager, Credit Operations, December 5, 1982, both at the Banco del Pacífico, Guayaquil.

8. Only six families (11 percent) built smaller components, such as bathrooms, foundations, and pillars.

9. See, for instance, Andrew Marshall Hamer, *Bogotá's Unregulated Subdivisions: The Myths and Realities of Incremental Housing Construction,* World Bank Staff Working Paper 734 (Washington, D.C., May 1985).

10. Interview with evaluators, Anop Pong Wat and Mitta Amnuay Unkammueng, Chiang Mai, April 16, 1984.

Chapter 5

1. The other three were for improving the garbage collection, cleaning up broken rock and debris left over from construction, and putting ornamental plants between the two cement paths which divided the rows of houses.

2. These men were typical; the forty-one renters surveyed in the upgraded area of 8 de Diciembre in April 1982 had lived an average of 6.4 years in the area.

3. The Bank project in Guayaquil did include a sites-and-services component;

people were to pay for land and infrastructure and build their houses as they wished, but the market for this component was largely unknown.

4. The rural immigrants in La Paz appeared to place far less importance on infrastructure than their counterparts in Guayaquil. This difference in opinion may be attributed to climatic factors; sanitation, water, and sewerage are perhaps more valued in the humid tropics than in the dry Altiplano.

5. Glenn Frankel, "Tanzania Symbolizes Failed Growth Model," *Washington Post,* November 19, 1984, pp. A1, A18–19.

Chapter 6

1. "Avaliação Qualitativa do Desenvolvimento da Pesca Artesanal no Rio Grande do Norte" (draft, May 1984), pp. 46–48 (my translation).

2. Qualitative interviews were done by staff of the evaluation units of project executing agencies in Bangkok (sites and services) and Florianópolis (milk cooperative).

Chapter 7

1. Michael H. Agar, *The Professional Stranger: An Informal Introduction to Ethnography* (New York: Academic Press, 1980).

2. George J. McCall and J. L. Simmons, *Issues in Participant Observation: A Text and Reader* (Reading, Mass.: Addison-Wesley, 1969), p. 1.

3. See Robert S. Weiss and Martin Rein, "The Evaluation of Broad-Aim Programs: Experimental Design, Its Difficulties and an Alternative," *Administrative Science Quarterly,* vol. 15, no. 1 (March 1970), pp. 97–109; and David Hamilton, "Evaluation as Illumination: A New Approach to the Study of Innovatory Programs," University of Edinburgh Centre for Research in the Educational Sciences, Occasional Paper 9, reprinted in G. V. Glass, ed., *Evaluation Studies Review Annual,* vol. 1 (Beverly Hills, Calif.: Sage, 1976).

4. Larissa Adler Lomnitz sees this lack of security as the major economic barrier to marginal urban populations (*Networks and Marginality: Life in a Mexican Shantytown* [New York: Academic Press, 1977], p. 208).

5. 3d ed., Chicago: University of Chicago Press, 1981, p. 303.

6. Michael Scriven, *Evaluation: A Study Guide for Educational Administrators* (Fort Lauderdale, Fla.: National Ed.D. Program for Educational Leaders, Nova University, 1978), p. 23.

7. See, for instance, Charles Reichardt and Thomas D. Cook, "Beyond Qualitative versus Quantitative Methods," in *Qualitative and Quantitative Methods in Evaluation Research* (Beverly Hills, Calif.: Sage, 1979), pp. 7–32; and Lee J. Cronbach, *Designing Evaluations of Educational and Social Programs* (San Francisco, Calif.: Jossey-Bass, 1982), pp. 301–10.

8. One particularly cogent critique of the exclusive reliance on questionnaire surveys, and a plea for complementary qualitative methods involving participant observation, is made by Linda Stone and J. Gabriel Campbell, "The Use and Misuse of Surveys in International Development: An Experiment from Nepal," *Human Organization,* vol. 43, no. 1 (Spring 1984), pp. 27–38.

9. Cronbach states that "goal attainment has received more emphasis in evaluation than it should," *Designing Evaluations*, p. 220. A more radical argument advocating "goal-free evaluation" is presented by Michael Scriven, "Pros and Cons about Goal-Free Evaluation," *Evaluation Comment*, vol. 1, no. 3 (Spring 1984), pp. 1–4.

10. *Reason in Common Sense* (New York: Dover, 1980), p. 222.

11. Beverly Hills, Calif.: Sage, 1982, pp. 118–19.

12. *Street Corner Society*, p. 300.

13. "Beyond ability, the informant's level and type of motivation affect performance in the interview. Genuine interest in the aims of the research is found to be the most efficacious motive." (John P. Dean and William Foote Whyte, "How Do You Know the Informant Is Telling the Truth?" in McCall and Simmons, *Issues in Participant Observation*, p. 115.)

14. The reference to friendship must be qualified because of the unusual nature of the bond between a participant observer and an informant. This issue is often discussed in the literature on participant observation with the caution to avoid overrapport, or getting so close to the informant that one loses the necessary critical and disinterested stance of the stranger (for further exploration of this issue, see McCall and Simmons, *Issues in Participant Observation*). On a different level, the nature of the friendship between observer and informant is affected by the different backgrounds of each and an awareness of the transitory nature of the observer's stay in the informant's community.

15. Boston: Little, Brown, 1967.

16. New York: Random, 1961.

17. See Whyte, *Street Corner Society*, p. 297: "There is a strain to doing such field work . . . Much as you enjoy your work, as long as you are observing and interviewing you have a role to play, and you are not completely relaxed."

18. A point made by many recent writers on evaluation. See, for example, Carol H. Weiss, "Increasing the Likelihood of Influencing Decisions," in Leonard Rutman, ed., *Evaluation Research Methods: A Basic Guide* (Beverly Hills, Calif.: Sage, 1984), p. 177; Cronbach, *Designing Evaluations*, p. 244; Patton, *Practical Evaluation*, p. 289.

19. This point is made by William Foote Whyte in his excellent recent book, *Learning from the Field: A Guide from Experience* (Beverly Hills, Calif.: Sage, 1984), p. 114. See also John P. Dean, Robert L. Eichorn, and Lois R. Dean, "Establishing Field Relations," in McCall and Simmons, *Issues in Participant Observation*, p. 73.

20. "Shortcut Methods of Gathering Social Information for Rural Development Projects," in Michael M. Cernea, ed., *Putting People First: Sociological Variables in Rural Development* (New York: Oxford University Press, 1985), pp. 403–04.

21. Norman Denzin, 1978, quoted in Michael Quinn Patton, *Qualitative Evaluation Methods* (Beverly Hills, Calif.: Sage, 1980), pp. 108–11. See also Whyte, *Learning from the Field*, p. 277.

22. "Statistical significance simply means that a given finding could not have occurred more than one time (or five times) out of a hundred on a chance basis, but this does not tell us whether what we are measuring is worth measuring" (Whyte, *Learning from the Field*, p. 231).

23. Patton describes various models and lists thirty-three types of evaluation; he stresses that model and type must give way to utility: "each evaluation setting is approached as a problem to be solved" (*Practical Evaluation*, pp. 37–49).

24. Michael H. Agar, "Toward an Ethnographic Language," *American Anthropologist*, vol. 84, no. 4 (December 1982), p. 783; and "Ethnographic Evidence," *Urban Life*, vol. 12, no. 1 (April 1983), pp. 33–34.

25. B. G. Glaser and A. L. Strauss, *The Discovery of Grounded Theory: Strategies for Qualitative Research* (Chicago, Ill.: Aldine, 1967), quoted in Whyte, *Learning from the Field*, p. 229.

26. W. S. Robinson, "The Logical Structure of Analytic Induction," in McCall and Simmons, *Issues in Participant Observation*, p. 199.

27. Malcomb Parlett and David Hamilton, "Evaluation as Illumination: A New Approach to the Study of Innovatory Programs," in Gene V. Glass, ed., *Evaluation Studies Review Annual*, vol. 1 (Beverly Hills, Calif.: Sage, 1976), pp. 140–57.

28. A point made by Weiss, "Increasing the Likelihood of Influencing Decisions," p. 179.

29. McCall and Simmons, *Issues in Participant Observation*, p. 341.

30. R. H. Wax, *Doing Field Work: Warnings and Advice* (Chicago, Ill.: University of Chicago Press, 1971), p. 365, quoted in Whyte, *Learning from the Field*, p. 104.

31. A recent study of surveys in Nepal found that for many rural Nepalese "the survey setting may be the *least* familiar and *least* comfortable context for providing personal information and expressing views." This study highlights the developmental significance of what is not said or is distorted in a questionnaire survey, and it recommends complementing this technique with qualitative methods such as participant observation, which bring out the context (Stone and Campbell, "The Use and Misuse of Surveys," pp. 29ff). For a cogent discussion of the importance of blending ethnographic and standard household approaches to determine income, see Susan Greenhalgh, "Income Units: The Ethnographic Alternative to Standardization," in Yoram Ben-Porath, ed., *Population and Development Review: Income Distribution and the Family* (New York: Population Council, 1982), pp. 70–91.

32. See, for instance, Romana P. de los Reyes, "Process Documentation: Social Science Research in a Learning Process Approach to Program Development," *Philippine Sociological Review*, vol. 32, no. 1–4 (January-December 1984), pp. 105–20.

33. There is a growing literature which should be referred to for more in-depth treatment than is offered here. A comprehensive reader on participant observation is the McCall and Simmons book, *Issues in Participant Observation*, referred to widely in this chapter. Particularly useful for a review of the methods of ethnography is Agar's *The Professional Stranger;* for the application of ethnography to field conditions, see Whyte's *Learning from the Field*. A thorough, historical review of various approaches to evaluation is Daniel L. Stufflebeam and Anthony J. Shinkfield, *Systematic Evaluation: A Self-Instructional Guide to Theory and Practice* (Boston, Mass.: Kluwer-Nijhoff, 1985). A work on evaluation, which, though not primarily oriented to international development projects, is consonant with the approach recommended here, is Patton's *Practical Evaluation*.

Chapter 8

1. New York: Harper and Row, 1982, pp. 77–78, 196.

C. Bibliography

Agar, Michael H. *The Professional Stranger: An Informal Introduction to Ethnography.* New York: Academic Press, 1980.

———. "Toward an Ethnographic Language." *American Anthropologist* 84, no. 4 (December 1982):779–96.

———. "Ethnographic Evidence." *Urban Life* 12, no. 1 (April 1983):32–49.

Albo, Xavier, Tomás Greaves, and Godofredo Sandoval. *Chukiyaqu, La Cara Aymara de La Paz: I. El Paso a la Ciudad.* CIPCA no. 20. La Paz, 1981.

Anderson, Dennis, and Farida Khambata. *Financing Small-Scale Industry and Agriculture in Developing Countries: The Merits and Limitations of "Commercial" Policies.* World Bank Staff Working Paper 519. Washington, D.C., 1982.

Arguello, G. "Evaluación de los Aspectos Técnicos del Plan Roldos de Vivienda Popular." Guayaquil: BEV-Unidad Ejecutora del Plan Emergente de Vivienda Popular, 1981.

Arteaga, Marcos. "Investigación de los Adjudicatarios del Plan Roldos de Vivienda Popular Respecto a los Niveles Social, Económico y Espacial en Su Situación Actual: Relación y Proyección Vivencial en Cuanto a la Unidad de Vivienda Adquirida." Guayaquil, March 1982.

Bamberger, Michael. "A Methodology for Impact Evaluation in Urban Shelter Programs." World Bank, Water Supply and Urban Development Department Discussion Paper 59. Washington, D.C., 1984.

Berger, Peter, and Thomas Luckmann. *The Social Construction of Reality: A Treatise in the Sociology of Knowledge.* New York: Doubleday, 1966.

Black, Philip A. "Participant Observation and Logical Positivism in the Social Sciences: A Note." *World Development* 11, no. 4 (April 1983):389–90.

Calderón G., Fernando, and Gonzalo Flores C. "Urbanización y Desarrollo: Necesidades Básicas en Areas Periféricas." UNICEF Serie Documentos no. 2. La Paz, April 1981.

Centro Pastoral-Arquidiócesis de La Paz. "La Opción por los Pobres: Algunos Datos Socio-Económicos de la Realidad Boliviana." La Paz, September 1979.

Cernea, Michael. "Indigenous Anthropologists and Development-Oriented Research." World Bank Reprint Series 208. In Hussein Fahim, ed., *Indigenous Anthropology in Non-Western Countries.* Durham, N.C.: Carolina Academic Press, 1982.

Cernea, Michael M., ed. *Putting People First: Sociological Variables in Rural Development.* New York: Oxford University Press, 1985.

Cronbach, Lee J. *Designing Evaluations of Educational and Social Programs.* San Francisco, Calif.: Jossey-Bass, 1982.

Davidoff, Paul, and Thomas Reiner. "A Choice Theory of Planning." *Journal of the American Institute of Planners* 28, no. 2 (May 1962):103–15.

de los Reyes, Romana P. "Process Documentation: Social Science Research in a Learning Process Approach to Program Development." *Philippine Sociological Review* 32, no. 1–4 (January-December 1984):105–20.

Deutscher, Irwin. "Toward Avoiding the Goal Trap in Evaluation Research." In Francis G. Caro, ed., *Readings in Evaluation Research*. New York: Russell Sage Foundation, 1977.

Etzioni, Amitai. "Mixed-Scanning: A 'Third' Approach to Decision-Making." *Public Administration Review* 27, no. 5 (December 1967):385–92.

Frankel, Barbara. "On Participant Observation as a Component of Evaluation: Strategies, Constraints and Issues." *Evaluation and Program Planning* 5, no. 3 (1982):239–47.

Friedrichs, Jurgen, and Harmut Ludtke. *Participant Observation: Theory and Practice*. Farnborough, Hants.: Saxon House, 1975.

Greenhalgh, Susan. "Income Units: The Ethnographic Alternative to Standardization." In Yoram Ben-Porath, ed., *Population and Development Review: Income Distribution and the Family*. New York: Population Council, 1982.

Geertz, Clifford. *The Interpretation of Cultures: Selected Essays*. New York: Basic Books, 1973.

Hamer, Andrew Marshall. *Bogotá's Unregulated Subdivisions: The Myths and Realities of Incremental Housing Construction*. World Bank Staff Working Paper 734. Washington, D.C., 1985.

Hamilton, David. "Evaluation as Illumination: A New Approach to the Study of Innovatory Programs." University of Edinburgh Centre for Research in the Educational Sciences, Occasional Paper 9. Reprinted in G. V. Glass, ed., *Evaluation Studies Review Annual*, vol. 1. Beverly Hills, Calif.: Sage, 1976.

Havens, Lester L. *Participant Observation*. New York: Jason Aronson, 1983.

Heidegger, Martin. *Basic Writings*. David Farrell Kress, ed. New York: Harper and Row, 1977.

Hirschman, Albert O. *Getting Ahead Collectively: Grassroots Experiences in Latin America*. New York: Pergamon, 1984.

Honorable Alcaldia Municipal de La Paz. *Plan de Desarrollo Urbano-Ciudad de La Paz*. La Paz, 1978.

Junta Nacional de la Vivienda–Banco Ecuatoriano de la Vivienda. "Plan Roldos de Vivienda Popular en Guayaquil." Guayaquil, 1981.

Kirk, Jerome, and Marc L. Miller. *Reliability and Validity in Qualitative Research*. Beverly Hills, Calif.: Sage, 1986.

Laporte, Bryce, and Roy Simon. "Urban Relocation and Family Adaptation in Puerto Rico: A Case Study in Urban Ethnography." In William Mangin, ed., *Peasants in Cities: Readings in the Anthropology of Urbanization*. Boston, Mass.: Houghton Mifflin, 1970.

Lee, Alfred McClung. "On Context and Relevance." In Glenn Jacobs, ed., *The Participant Observer*. New York: Braziller, 1970.

Leeds, Anthony. "'Subjective' and 'Objective' in Social Anthropological Epistemology." In R. J. Seeger and R. S. Cohen, eds., *Philosophical Foundations of Science*. Boston Studies in the Philosophy of Science, vol. 11. Dordrecht, Holland: D. Reidel, 1984.

Lewis, Oscar. *The Children of Sánchez*. New York: Random, 1961.

————. *La Vida: A Puerto Rican Family in the Culture of Poverty.* New York: Random, 1965.

Liebow, Elliot. *Tally's Corner.* Boston, Mass.: Little, Brown, 1967.

Linn, Johannes F. *Cities in the Developing World: Policies for Their Equitable and Efficient Growth.* New York: Oxford University Press, 1983.

Lloyd, Peter. *Slums of Hope? Shantytowns of the Third World.* New York: St. Martin's, 1979.

Loizos, Peter. *The Heart Grown Bitter.* Cambridge, Eng.: Cambridge University Press, 1981.

Lomnitz, Larissa Adler. *Networks and Marginality: Life in a Mexican Shantytown.* New York: Academic, 1977.

Luzuriaga, Carlos. "Issues of Human Settlements in Ecuador." USAID Mission in Ecuador, November 1980.

McCall, George J., and J. L. Simmons, eds. *Issues in Participant-Observation: A Text and Reader.* Reading, Mass.: Addison-Wesley, 1969.

Middleton, Alan. "Class Power and the Distribution of Credit in Ecuador." *Bulletin of the Society for Latin American Studies,* no. 33 (April 1981):66–100.

Mirabella, Giovanni C., Gloria Ardaya, and others. "Factores Psicosociales de la Migración Rural-Urbana." La Paz: Centro de Estudios de la Realidad Económica y Social (CERES), October 1980.

Moore, Richard James Thomas. "Assimilation and Political Participation among the Poor in Guayaquil, Ecuador." Ph.D. diss., University of Texas at Austin, 1977.

Moser, Caroline O. N. "A Home of One's Own: Squatter Housing Strategies in Guayaquil, Ecuador." In Alan Gilbert and others, eds., *Urbanization in Contemporary Latin America: Critical Approaches to the Analysis of Urban Issues.* New York: Wiley, 1982.

Parlett, Malcomb, and David Hamilton. "Evaluation as Illumination: A New Approach to the Study of Innovatory Programs." In G. V. Glass, ed., *Evaluation Studies Review Annual,* vol. 1. Beverly Hills, Calif.: Sage, 1976.

Patton, Michael Quinn. *Qualitative Evaluation Methods.* Beverly Hills, Calif.: Sage, 1980.

————. *Practical Evaluation.* Beverly Hills, Calif.: Sage, 1982.

Peattie, Lisa Redfield. *The View from the Barrio.* Ann Arbor, Mich.: University of Michigan Press, 1968.

Peters, Thomas J., and Robert H. Waterman. *In Search of Excellence: Lessons from America's Best-Run Companies.* New York: Warner, 1982.

Ponce, Alicia, and Hernán Valencia. "Configuración del Espacio Regional Ecuatoriano y Desarrollo Urbano de Quito y Guayaquil." Documento HABQUI, no. 19. Paper prepared for the third seminar on African–Latin American Precarious Human Settlements, Quito, October 1981.

Raiffa, Howard. *Decision Analysis: Introductory Lectures on Choices under Uncertainty.* Reading, Mass.: Addison-Wesley, 1968.

Reichardt, Charles S., and Thomas D. Cook, eds. *Qualitative and Quantitative Methods in Evaluation Research.* Beverly Hills, Calif.: Sage, 1979.

Rivera, Alberto. "Pachamama Expensive: El Contexto Territorial Urbano y la Diferenciación Social en la Ciudad de la Paz, 1971–1976." La Paz: Centro de Estudios de la Realidad Económica y Social (CERES), October 1981.

Rodríguez, Alfredo. "Notas para el Análisis del Suburbio y Tugurio de Guayaquil." *Revista Interamericana de Planificación* 19, no. 54 (June 1980):142–59.

Rosero, Fernando, Martha Moscoso, and Arturo Maldonado. "Investigación Socio-Económica de los Barrios Suburbanos de Guayaquil." Quito: Ministerio de Bienestar Social y Promoción Popular, July 1981.

Salomón, Jorge. "El Problema de la Vivienda en Guayaquil: Implicaciones y Soluciones." Guayaquil, August 25, 1982.

―――. "Estudio Socio-Económico de Guasmo Norte." Municipality of Guayaquil, October 1981.

―――. "Descripción de las Reuniones de la Comunidad en Guasmo Norte." Guayaquil: Municipal Executing Unit, February 1980.

Sandoval, Godofredo, and Xavier Albo. *Ojje por Encima de Todo: Historia de un Centro de Residentes Ex-Campesinas en La Paz.* La Paz: CIPCA, 1978.

Santayana, George. *Reason in Common Sense.* "The Life of Reason," vol. 1. New York: Dover, 1980.

Schatzman, Leonard, and Anselm L. Strauss. *Field Research: Strategies for a Natural Sociology.* Englewood Cliffs, N.J.: Prentice-Hall, 1973.

Schwartzmann, Helen B. "The Ethnographic Evaluation of Human Services Programs: Guidelines and an Illustration." *Anthropological Quarterly* 56, no. 4 (October 1983):179–89.

Scriven, Michael. "Pros and Cons about Goal-Free Evaluation." *Evaluation Comment* 1, no. 3 (1972):1–4.

―――. *Evaluation: A Study Guide for Educational Administrators.* Fort Lauderdale, Fla.: National Ed.D. Program for Educational Leaders, Nova University, 1974.

Spradley, James P. *Participant Observation.* New York: Holt, Rinehart, and Winston, 1980.

Stone, Linda, and J. Gabriel Campbell. "The Use and Misuse of Surveys in International Development: An Experiment from Nepal." *Human Organization* 43, no. 1 (Spring 1984):27–38.

Strassman, W. Paul. *The Transformation of Urban Housing: The Experience of Upgrading in Cartagena.* Baltimore, Md.: Johns Hopkins University Press, 1982.

Stufflebeam, Daniel L., and Anthony J. Shinkfield. *Systematic Evaluation: A Self-Instructional Guide to Theory and Practice.* Boston, Mass.: Kluwer-Nijhoff, 1985.

Unidad Ejecutora Municipal, Departamento Social. "Síntesis del Primer Proyecto de Desarrollo Urbano de Guayaquil." Guayaquil, February 1982.

Van Maanen, John, ed. "Reclaiming Qualitative Methods for Organizational Research: A Preface." *Administrative Science Quarterly* 24 (December 1979):520–26.

―――. "The Fact of Friction in Organizational Ethnography." *Administrative Science Quarterly* 24 (December 1979):539–50.

Villavicencio, Gaitán. "La Política de Vivienda de los Gobiernos de las Fuerzas Armadas Ecuatorianas (1972–77): Elementos para una Discusión." Quito, March 1981.

———. "Democracia, Populismo y Lucha: Reindicativas Urbanas: El Caso de Guayaquil (La Lucha por la Tierra y la Vivienda, 1978–1979)." In *Explotación y Miseria Urbana: La Lucha por la Tierra y la Vivienda en Guayaquil.* Guayaquil: Instituto de Investigaciones Económicas y Políticas, Universidad de Guayaquil, November 1980.

Villavicencio, Gaitán, and Diego Carrión. "Acciones de los Sectores Populares Frente al Problema de la Tierra Urbana y Reacciones de las Fuerzas Socio-Políticas Afectadas: El Caso de Quito y Guayaquil." Documento HABQUI, no. 30. Paper prepared for the third seminar on African–Latin American Precarious Human Settlements, Quito, October 1981.

Webb, Eugene J., and Donald T. Campbell. *Nonreactive Measures in the Social Sciences.* 2d ed. Boston, Mass.: Houghton Mifflin, 1981.

Weiss, Carol H. "Increasing the Likelihood of Influencing Decisions." In Leonard Rutman, ed., *Evaluation Research Methods: A Basic Guide.* Beverly Hills, Calif.: Sage, 1984.

Weiss, Robert S., and Martin Rein. "The Evaluation of Broad-Aim Programs: Experimental Design, Its Difficulties and an Alternative." *Administrative Science Quarterly* 15, no. 1 (March 1970), pp. 97–109.

Whyte, William Foote. *Street Corner Society: The Social Structure of an Italian Slum.* 3d ed., Chicago, Ill.: University of Chicago Press, 1981.

———. *Learning from the Field: A Guide from Experience.* Beverly Hills, Calif.: Sage, 1984.

Williams, David D., ed. "Naturalistic Evaluation." *New Directions for Program Evaluation,* no. 30 (1986).

World Bank. *Learning by Doing: World Bank Lending for Urban Development, 1972–82.* Washington, D.C., 1983.

INDEX